BRIDGE:
WINNING WAYS TO PLAY YOUR CARDS

BRIDGE: WINNING WAYS TO PLAY YOUR CARDS

Paul Mendelson

A HOW TO BOOK

ROBINSON

ROBINSON

First published in Great Britain in 2005 as *Bridge: Play Your Cards Right*

This edition published in 2008 by Robinson

A CIP catalogue record for this book
is available from the British Library.

ISBN 978-0-7160-2197-1

Printed and bound in Great Britain by Clays Ltd., St Ives plc

Papers used by Robinson are from well-managed forests
and other responsible sources

MIX
Paper from
responsible sources
FSC
www.fsc.org   FSC® C104740

Robinson
An imprint of
Little, Brown Book Group
Carmelite House
50 Victoria Embankment
London EC4Y 0DZ

An Hachette UK Company
www.hachette.co.uk

www.littlebrown.co.uk

How To Books are published by Robinson, an imprint of Little, Brown Book Group.
We welcome proposals from authors who have first-hand experience of their subjects.
Please set out the aims of your book, its target market and its suggested contents in
an email to Nikki.Read@howtobooks.co.uk

CONTENTS

INTRODUCTION

Every week, in my work for *The Financial Times*, I am sent a great pile of bridge handbooks to review. The hands illustrated are magical and inspiring, making for great journalism but, all too often, they are illustrations of plays that you will probably never see again. In *Winning Ways To Play Your Cards*, I want to focus on the type of hands which crop up every time you play, the class of hands which will make a real difference to your scores, the type which, once mastered, will be the springboard for real improvement in your game.

Wherever you play bridge – especially social rubber bridge – it is your card-play which will account for most of your success. Even if your bidding were perfect, play and defence will net you many more points over the years.

Both as declarer and as a defender, you need an effective strategy in order to play your cards right. Often these strategies are mirror-images of one another. For that is the key to successful card-play: if the declarer has one plan, the defenders must counter it with one of their own. You cannot properly consider your own strategy in isolation from that of your opponents. For every thought they have, you need to have a counter, and vice versa. This is how it must happen in real life, at the table, and here, in *Winning Ways To Play Your Cards*, you have a book which will help you to think in exactly that way.

Once you have identified the main lines of play for the declarer, both at no-trumps and with a trump suit, the more adept you will become at thinking ahead strategically. As those skills improve, your appreciation of what is going on in all four hands around the table will improve more than you ever dreamt possible.

In no-trump contracts, both the declarer and defender have identical aims: to establish enough winners to foil their opponents. The play in no-trumps is a race, plain and simple, but it is not necessarily a sprint. It is a cross-country course, full of potential for tactics as well as for sheer speed.

In suit contracts, the strategy to be employed by declarer will usually depend upon the shape of the dummy hand. Declarer must establish a long suit or ruff losers there and, failing that, he should look for finesses, endplays or squeezes. Defending, you must counter each of these moves and, if possible, anticipate the declarer's strategy and attack him from trick one.

Overall, it is important to appreciate that the declarer can adopt only relatively few lines of play and that your defence needs to concentrate upon blocking whichever of these declarer may deploy.

The auction provides vital clues for both declarer and defenders. To decipher the true meanings of bids, leads and early defence, and to construct a picture of your opponents' cards will help you to plan your campaign. This will involve counting and card-reading for the declarer; and the use of signals and discards to impart information between defenders.

Many of these techniques will be best learnt with your regular playing partner or group, so that you can introduce them to your game and suffer minimum complications whilst doing so. However, in order to improve you must not shy away from the best players in your club or circle. Rather, you should relish every opportunity to face the best players in order to hone your own game. With this combination of learning and experience, your confidence will increase, your results will improve, your reputation will become stronger and your brain will be ready to tackle still more expert techniques. It is a fantastic positive upward spiral . . .

As you see each of the examples, you may be tempted to speed-read your way through the early ones. I urge you, however, to take your time and be certain that you understand the fundamental principles because these are the steps without which you cannot climb. If you are not confident of a technique, grab a pack of cards, lay out the hand and play it through. This can cement a principle for life.

Sometimes, during an explanation of the course of play, you'll be able to observe as a spectator. Sometimes, you will be placed in the driving seat and asked to make decisions. If you can, try to resist the urge to skip ahead to find the answer, and instead work it out for yourself. Without doubt, you will learn more by doing so.

To my mind, bridge is not about rules. It is a game where, as time passes and your experience widens, your understanding of the complexities grows. This book sets out to take you through years of experience, smoothly and without grouchy comments from your partner or opponents, to enrich your understanding of the key principles and to set you on a path where nothing at the green baize is a secret. Instead, anything new should simply fire your enthusiasm for understanding and learning from it.

Quite often when I play, a smile comes over my face. It is the recognition that I face a problem and I am not yet sure how to solve it. I play for moments like these. It is a great feeling when, as you truly start to influence what happens, and your play proves equal to the task, the cards start working with you and everything comes together perfectly.

You will also notice in the examples that your opponents do not always bid as you would have done. You must cope with that and derive whatever information you can from their auction; that is exactly how it is in real life.

Finally, as usual, I have made the players at the table male – they are all he and not she. In our conservation-aware times, you will appreciate that this represents a massive saving on S's and the ink required to print them.

Paul Mendelson
London

1
KEY STRATEGY FOR SUIT CONTRACTS

The moment a hand of bridge is dealt, the two partnerships begin to jostle for position. During both bidding and play, when one side takes action, the other endeavours to counter it – and the action taken cannot be random: it must be a direct response to the aims and strategies of the opposing side.

The overriding fact to grasp about suit contracts, whether you are the declarer or in defence is that, for declarer to succeed, there are only three basic strategies he will be able to adopt:

- Ruffing losers in dummy.
- Establishing a long suit in dummy or, rarely, in his own hand.
- Relying on finesses, endplays, and defensive errors.

The declarer must decide which of these options to take and, to succeed, the defence must identify the strategy and seek to counter it directly.

Sometimes, in defence, you will be able to assess which line the declarer is likely to take just from the auction; at other times, you will need to see the dummy [hand] before feeling confident about what plan your opponent may have. On rare occasions, you may even need to wait to see declarer's early play before being able to launch your counter-offensive. But counter-attack you must and, nineteen times out of twenty, you should respond to his basic strategy as follows:

- If dummy contains shortages of which declarer may wish to take advantage for making ruffs, lead trumps to cut down dummy's ruffing potential.
- Indeed, whenever declarer hesitates before pulling trumps, your thoughts should be on leading them.
- If dummy contains a long, establishable suit, attack the other non-trump suits aggressively, so that declarer will not have time to throw his losers away on dummy's winning tricks.
- If dummy is relatively balanced (which accounts for most hands), defend as safely as possible, so that you neither open up new suits nor provide declarer with free finesses. A forcing defence, as will be described in Chapter 3 – making declarer trump in his own hand – usually works very effectively.

Understanding that in a suit contract declarer has just three basic strategies from which to choose, and the counter-offensives appropriate to each of them, will help you to find the best line, both as declarer and defender, on the vast majority of occasions. In the chapters that follow, all kinds of variations on this theme will be examined but one, simple, underlying philosophy remains constant: identify your opponents' strategy and then counter it directly.

To set the mood let's take a look, with this understanding, at a few examples and how you set about countering your opponents' plans.

Pay careful attention during the auction because, especially if you end up defending, the very progress of the bidding may tip you off as to the likely shape of dummy and therefore to declarer's probable plan. If you remain uncertain as to why the defensive line would succeed, take time to lay out and play out the deal so that you can see how the strategy succeeds in beating the declarer's planned route.

Interpreting the Auction

Hand 1   Dealer South

N	E	S	W
–	–	1H	NB
2H	NB	3H	NB
4H			

This is a typical, social rubber bridge auction where, probably, both North and South have stretched the values required for their bids. However, all too often, this type of bidding leads to a making contract. How do you, as East-West, suppose that declarer will scramble ten tricks? Almost certainly, North-South do not hold sufficient points between them to make game just on high-card strength; nor is there any evidence of an establishable suit. So, it looks like ruffing, and possibly cross-ruffing, will be declarer's only hope. As a defender, this auction screams for a trump lead, so you can attack declarer's best asset immediately.

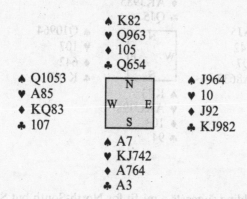

South faces five losers: the ace of trumps, three diamonds and a club. If South can ruff two diamonds in dummy, his troubles are over and, without a trump lead, this can be achieved easily. However, if West interprets the auction correctly, he will lead A♥ followed by a low heart and, when he regains the lead with a

high diamond, he can shoot through a third trump, leaving
dummy one trump short. Declarer will hope that West holds K♣
but, when East beats dummy's Q♣, the contract is defeated.

For West, there are several other attractive opening leads – but
each would have led to South succeeding in his game. A low
spade or K♦ are both quite acceptable – though a doubleton
club certainly is not (see page 78). However, here, the auction
should guide West to the killing trump lead.

Hand 2   **Dealer South**

N	E	S	W
–	–	1H	NB
2D	NB	2H	NB
3D	NB	**4H**	

```
                    ♠ 82
                    ♥ 63
                    ♦ AKJ985
                    ♣ QJ5
      ♠ AJ5        ┌─────────┐      ♠ Q10964
      ♥ 542        │    N    │      ♥ 107
      ♦ Q7         │ W     E │      ♦ 642
      ♣ A8632      │    S    │      ♣ K107
                   └─────────┘
                    ♠ K73
                    ♥ AKQJ98
                    ♦ 103
                    ♣ 94
```

The early bidding suggests a misfit for North-South but South's
final jump to 4H should warn you, as defenders, that his trumps
are high quality. If dummy's diamonds are either solid or
establishable, their contract is likely to be secure unless you can
cash your winners quickly, before declarer throws his losers away
on dummy's diamonds. This is the time to make a really attacking lead, because there is an urgency to take your tricks.

Since you know that dummy contains a long, good quality diamond suit, your own meagre holding of ♦Q7 suggests that declarer will have no problem in establishing that suit to provide discards of losing cards from his hand.

A black suit lead, to facilitate taking your tricks quickly, is strongly suggested. Against a suit contract, to lead an unsupported ace, or to lead a small card away from a suit headed by an ace, would be highly risky and likely to give away tricks (see page 84). However, the auction demands that you attack the unbid suits.

Holding ♠AJ5, you may prefer a spade lead from your partner, through the declarer's hand, to capture any honour he may hold there. So, a club seems best. The lead of A♣ allows you to view dummy and receive a signal (page 91) from partner. East should encourage you to continue leading clubs and, when he gains the lead with K♣, he should be equally aware of the threat from dummy's diamonds and he should switch to a spade, probably 10♠. Declarer must now lose four tricks and be defeated.

Notice that if you had made a passive lead, such as a trump, South would have pulled trumps and run his diamonds, pitching four black-suit losers from his hand, ending up with twelve tricks. The auction provided you with sufficient information to decide on an attacking lead – and you were never getting a second chance.

Both these auctions and contracts required decisive, positive action in order to counter them. Sadly, however, defence against suit contracts is more often a very unglamorous, unsexy pastime, where discipline and order are key and snazzy plays have no place. Whenever dummy is relatively balanced, your initial aim in defence will be to avoid giving tricks away. If both declarer's and dummy's hand turn out to lack shape, then your entire defence will be about just that. In simple terms, if declarer cannot ruff in dummy, or establish a long suit, he will either have to form some complicated manoeuvre or endplay, keep his fingers crossed on finesses, or rely on the defence giving him his contract. In this situation, if you can defend in a passive or neutral style, this will give declarer the most problems.

Hand 3   Dealer South

N	E	S	W
–	–	1H	NB
2NT	NB	4H	

Another familiar, simple auction but one which tips you off that dummy is likely to be flat, suggesting a passive defence. It looks as if declarer will have to work for his tricks, so you must not help him. Select a safe, neutral lead (see page 79) and make him work every step of the way.

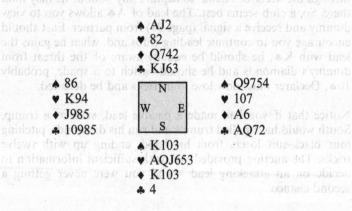

```
              ♠ AJ2
              ♥ 82
              ◆ Q742
              ♣ KJ63
   ♠ 86            N         ♠ Q9754
   ♥ K94       W     E       ♥ 107
   ◆ J985                    ◆ A6
   ♣ 10985          S        ♣ AQ72
              ♠ K103
              ♥ AQJ653
              ◆ K103
              ♣ 4
```

This is a typical tight contract: declarer faces a club loser, two diamond losers, a trump, and a two-way finesse in spades. As West, you must not be tempted to make an aggressive lead (see page 77), such as a low diamond or doubleton spade, since either immediately presents declarer with an extra trick. A low trump lead would be safe, although there is little possibility that ruffs are possible in dummy. The most passive lead, however, is the top-of-sequence 10♣ which is highly unlikely to cost your side extra tricks. Now, the fate of the contract is in the balance.

Assuming that South covers 10♣ with an honour from dummy, East will win the trick, and should realise that he must wait to have clubs led to him again. That accepted, what switch looks safe? A spade solves declarer's problems there, ace and another diamond enables declarer to reduce his two diamond losers to one. Only a trump is safe for West. Declarer probably finesses, West wins with K♥ and leads 9♣. Declarer trumps that trick and, whenever they regain the lead, East-West continue playing clubs, making South ruff in hand with trump tricks he would make at the end anyway, and leaving him to guess the spade and diamond positions. Only in the highly unlikely scenario that South guesses who holds Q♠ and works out that East holds a doubleton ♦Ax will he prevail . . . unless you help him.

This type of contract is regularly allowed to be made when defenders get too aggressive and switch from suit to suit, looking for tricks. When defending, you almost never look for tricks – you wait to take them when it will cause maximum damage to the declarer and not before.

So, the content of your opponents' auction may provide vital clues to get you off to the best start in defence. Even their style and tone may have a bearing on how you defend:

If your opponents' auction is confident and they appear to have sufficient high-card points for their contract, make an aggressive lead (see page 77). Such leads will include singletons and leads away from honours.

If your opponents' auction seems stretched and high-card points may be lacking, defend passively, take no risks, and wait for your own winners to defeat the contract. Opt for a trump lead or top-of-sequence honour card.

2

SUIT CONTRACTS – FOCUS ON DECLARER PLAY

When playing a suit contract, your basic strategy is to count the losers you hold in your own hand, taking into account any winners in dummy. Finesses should be counted as losers, so that you force yourself to seek a superior line than a 50% bet. Cards which need to be ruffed in dummy must also be counted as losers, since your plan must include making those ruffs.

Having assessed the number of losing cards in hand, you must plan to dispose of as many as are required to succeed. This will involve ruffing in dummy or establishing a long suit. If this does not work, there may be a more complex play such as an endplay or squeeze, or you may simply have to rely upon luck in terms of finesses and defensive errors.

Instead of counting losers, some players may prefer to count their tricks. Certainly this works well when you hold only seven trumps, or the trump split is poor. But, whether you look for tricks or losers, you still have to deal with them.

Do not touch that first card from dummy until you have decided which strategy to adopt. Even if you sit as the sky darkens and night sets in, do not be tempted to play to the first trick and then make a plan. In fact, let your opponents mummify before playing too quickly. At first, you may be subjected to tapping of fingers and glancing at time-pieces but, if you persist, your analysis will speed up and your results will shame your opponents into taking similar care as defenders in assessing the potential of dummy and declarer's hand together.

Later, we will examine the significance of the opponents' bidding – or lack of it – and that will add a further dimension to your early thoughts but, for now, let us examine some of the fundamental plays and develop the skills from simple hands to more complex challenges.

Drawing Trumps

If you have few enough losers (or enough tricks) to make your contract, draw trumps as soon as possible. If you do not require them in dummy, either for ruffing or as entries during a suit establishment, then it is safer to pull them out of your opponents' hands.

Hand 4   Dealer North

N	E	S	W
1NT	NB	4S	

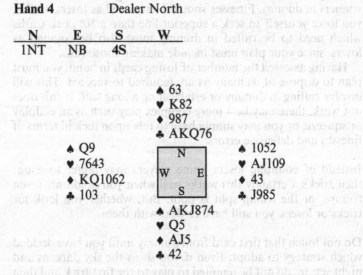

```
                    ♠ 63
                    ♥ K82
                    ♦ 987
                    ♣ AKQ76
   ♠ Q9          ┌─────────┐      ♠ 1052
   ♥ 7643        │    N    │      ♥ AJ109
   ♦ KQ1062      │ W     E │      ♦ 43
   ♣ 103         │    S    │      ♣ J985
                 └─────────┘
                    ♠ AKJ874
                    ♥ Q5
                    ♦ AJ5
                    ♣ 42
```

Let's take a moment to count those losers properly. Work through each suit in turn, assessing where you will lose tricks. In spades, you are missing the queen, which counts as one loser. You have eight spades between the two hands, so you should not need to worry about losing the 10♠ (although really poor distribution always has the potential to destroy the best-laid plans). In hearts, dummy's king and your queen mean that you have only the ace to lose. In diamonds, you are missing both king and queen and dummy's holding does not help you, so that is two losers. Finally, in clubs, your own hand contains two losers but dummy's ♣AKQ will cover those and provide a discard for another loser as well.

In total then, you have four losers: one spade, one heart and two diamonds, but you have an easy discard on the third top club, which will allow you to pitch a diamond loser from hand once trumps are drawn.

How should you plan the play of the hand?
West leads K♦ and you decide to win. Many would now cash a top trump and then cross to dummy to take the finesse. However, this line results in defeat as West wins, cashes Q♦, provides a ruff for East, and then waits for East's A♥ to kill the contract.

South holds four losers, but he can pitch a diamond loser on the clubs. Therefore, South has few enough losers (or enough winners) to make 4S so he should draw the trumps as quickly as possible.

The winning line is to take trick one, cash ♠AK and then, if Q♠ has not fallen, to start playing clubs, planning to pitch a diamond loser on the third round. On this hand, West's Q♠ falls doubleton, so now South can draw the final trump also before cashing ♣AKQ and claiming his contract.

So, when you have sufficient tricks to secure your contract, pull trumps quickly – and that may well include refusing finesses (you have counted them as losers anyway) and laying down top cards to remove enemy trumps fast.

Drawing the Final Trump
When it comes to pulling an opponent's final trump, it is usually right to do this when you will then have enough tricks to secure your contract, and when to allow your opponent to ruff in with his final trump might disrupt your cashing of those tricks.

Hand 5   Dealer North

N	E	S	W
1D	NB	1S	NB
2S	NB	**4S**	

```
                    ♠ 762
                    ♥ Q2
                    ♦ AKQJ83
                    ♣ 42
     ♠ 4                           ♠ J1098
     ♥ AKJ7          N             ♥ 108543
     ♦ 1096       W     E          ♦ 5
     ♣ QJ1097        S             ♣ 863
                    ♠ AKQ53
                    ♥ 96
                    ♦ 742
                    ♣ AK5
```

West leads ♥AK and realises that, with a threatening suit in dummy, he must continue to attack the remaining suits aggressively. The Q♣ switch is marked anyway being top-of-a-sequence and South wins with his A♣.

The only danger here is if trumps split badly and declarer does not remain alert. Despite the fact that this is an easy hand with plenty of tricks, many declarers fail because, mentally, they are already chalking up the game score, and they fail to adjust when the news is bad.

Here, South plays two rounds of trumps before discovering the bad break. Should he continue with trumps or start on diamonds? Since his club loser is still protected by a top honour, he must pull the remaining trump or risk being cut off from dummy and the ability to pitch his club loser on a diamond. He cashes Q♠ and then loses the fourth round to East. Whatever East returns, declarer can win, and then run his diamond suit.

If he were to play on diamonds rather than pulling the final trump, East would wait until South would be void in diamonds and ruff the third round, and lead a club. Declarer would be in hand and unable to return to dummy to enjoy the diamond winners.

Trump Control – Countering a Forcing Defence

When you are short of trumps, it may be necessary to lose a trump trick early on while you retain control of all the suits. This is especially the case when you are likely to be subjected to a forcing defence. This next hand may seem tough but, once you learn to foresee the likely actions of your opponents, the methods to foil them will come to you more readily.

Hand 6   Dealer East

N	E	S	W
–	NB	1H	NB
1NT	NB	4H	

```
                      ♠ 965
                      ♥ 84
                      ♦ 984
                      ♣ AQ863
        ♠ K10          ┌─────────┐    ♠ J8432
        ♥ J763         │    N    │    ♥ 52
        ♦ KQ1062       │ W     E │    ♦ AJ5
        ♣ 95           │    S    │    ♣ 1074
                       └─────────┘
                      ♠ AQ7
                      ♥ AKQ109
                      ♦ 73
                      ♣ KJ2
```

Although 3NT fails on a diamond lead, if South had raised North to 3NT immediately, East would probably have led a spade and declarer could have grabbed a spade, three heart and five club tricks before the defence re-gained the lead. However, wary of his small doubleton diamond and seduced by his solid-looking hearts (and, being an old-fashioned rubber bridge player, the accompanying one hundred points for honours) South punted game in hearts. It was to be only his first mistake . . .

West led K♦ and followed it up with a low one to East's A♦. East played a third round and South ruffed. Now, South played three top trumps and discovered the bad break. With no other entry to dummy other than clubs, he resigned himself to finding West with three clubs as well as the last trump and played that suit. However, West trumped in on the third round and led a fourth diamond – a classic forcing manoeuvre, forcing declarer to trump with his long holding and therefore reducing his trump length and control of the hand. Here, South was compelled to use his final trump. Now, unable to reach dummy's winning clubs, declarer had to lose to West's K♠ and he received a fifth diamond to defeat him by two tricks. Could he have done better?

A 3–3 trump break has a 31.25% – or a 1 in 3 – chance (see page 42) so declarer should expect a poor break. Since he is short of trumps, he should foresee the prospect of more diamonds being led to reduce his holding still further. If he still held a trump in dummy, his opponents could not lead diamonds profitably, since he would be able to ruff in dummy and preserve his trump length in hand. The solution: at trick four, having trumped the third round of diamonds in hand, he plays a **low** trump from hand and gives up his likely trump loser now. In fact, West may be so surprised by the sight of a low trump, he may duck – assuming that his partner can win – and squander his trick altogether. Assuming, however, that West does win, he is stymied; he cannot profitably lead another diamond. (If he does, South ruffs in dummy, returns to hand with a top club and draws all three rounds of trumps. Then he runs his clubs, pitching both spade losers from hand.) If West leads another suit, declarer can win, pull the trumps and take his spade discards on the long club suit.

From a defensive point of view, you do not want to leave yourself with a singleton top trump. In that situation, declarer will be most unlikely to waste his trumps simply to lose to your master trump. Generally, then, you should take your master trump earlier on, and then continue with trumps, or find an appropriate switch.

Trump Control – Preserving your Trump Quality
If you have plenty of points for your contract and enough tricks seem accessible, you may find that your opponents attempt to promote their own modest trumps into winners, by making you trump high – as you will see in the defence section, page 88. You

must be alert to preserve your trump quality, utilizing an important counter.

Hand 7   Dealer South

N	E	S	W
–	–	1S	2D
2S	NB	4S	

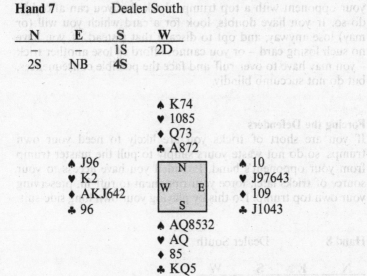

```
                 ♠ K74
                 ♥ 1085
                 ♦ Q73
                 ♣ A872
   ♠ J96          N          ♠ 10
   ♥ K2                      ♥ J97643
   ♦ AKJ642    W     E       ♦ 109
   ♣ 96           S          ♣ J1043
                 ♠ AQ8532
                 ♥ AQ
                 ♦ 85
                 ♣ KQ5
```

West leads ♦AK and receives an encouraging peter (see page 91) from East. Since East is most unlikely to hold a defensive trick (West has 12pts and North-South are likely to have 26pts between them to be in a confidently bid game contract), West decides that together with his K♥, he might be able to promote his J♠ into a trick if he can make declarer ruff with a top trump in his hand. To this end, West leads a third diamond, dummy plays Q♦ and East ruffs with 10♠. If South now over-ruffs with Q♠, he will be defeated. With only ♠AK left, West's J♠ will score on the third round and South's heart finesse will lose also, resulting in defeat.

The solution is simple. Since South should have counted all finesses as losers, he should have viewed his Q♥ with distain. Instead of over-ruffing with Q♠ and running the risk of setting up a trump trick for the defence, he discards Q♥ instead. Whatever East leads now, declarer can win, draw trumps and claim his contract. This is a classic "loser-on-loser" play.

Your opponents will frequently seek to promote their trumps, so be aware. Whenever you are offered the opportunity to over-ruff your opponent with a top trump, check that you can afford to do so. If you have doubts, look for a card which you will (or may) lose anyway, and opt to discard that instead. If you have no such losing card – or you cannot afford to lose another trick – you may have to over-ruff and face the possible consequences, but do not succumb blindly.

Forcing the Defenders

If you are short of tricks you are likely to need your own trumps, so do not waste yours simply to pull the master trump from your opponent's hand. Provided you have access to your source of tricks later, force your opponent to ruff in, preserving your own top trump. Do this by playing your own long side-suit.

Hand 8   Dealer South

N	E	S	W
–	–	1S	NB
2C	NB	2D	NB
2S	NB	4S	

♠ 97
♥ J73
♦ AJ5
♣ QJ732

♠ J532   ♠ 84
♥ KQ1064   ♥ A982
♦ 98   ♦ KQ62
♣ 84   ♣ 1095

♠ AKQ106
♥ 5
♦ 10743
♣ AK6

This auction is not a thing of beauty, but the result is the game with the best chance of making. Unlike hand 6, there is a side-entry to dummy's long suit, and this allows declarer to take active control of the hand.

West leads K♥ and, when this holds, he continues with a low heart to East's ace. South ruffs and plays three rounds of trumps, again finding them dividing 4–2. This time, re-assured that he can return to dummy with A♦ later, he should ignore West's last trump and begin to play on clubs. Whenever West decides to trump in, declarer is still in control. Having trumped, if West plays a third heart, declarer can trump with his last spade and continue playing his club winners, using A♦ as an entry to dummy if required. Two of his diamond losers are discarded on the winning clubs and the contract succeeds.

    If, instead, South unthinkingly draws West's last trump, West simply cashes three more heart winners since South has run out of trumps.

Not Drawing Trumps

The two main occasions when you would not draw trumps immediately are as follows:

- When you need them for ruffing losers in dummy.
- When you need them as entries to reach dummy and, occasionally, to reach your own hand.

Let's identify these situations and put the tactics into action, starting with simple examples and developing the themes.

Cross-Ruffing

When neither declarer nor dummy holds a long suit, but both hands contain shortages, look for an opportunity to ruff in dummy, and also use ruffs in your own hand as a means of returning to hand. This is the classic cross-ruff.

Hand 9   Dealer South

N	E	S	W
–	–	1S	NB
3S	NB	4S	

♠ Q1074
♥ 8
♦ A643
♣ A852

♠ 2	♠ J93
♥ KQJ10	♥ 9652
♦ J975	♦ Q10
♣ K1064	♣ QJ97

♠ AK865
♥ A743
♦ K82
♣ 3

West leads K♥ and South sees that he holds three heart losers and a diamond loser. To succeed, he needs only to ruff one losing heart in dummy. This will provide his tenth trick. However, to make the maximum number of tricks, he can aim to ruff all his heart losers in dummy, using his own club shortage as a means of access back to hand. Notice that declarer has no other long suit which will produce tricks – his trumps must be used separately to make the most of them.

Winning K♥ with A♥, South ruffs a heart in dummy and cashes A♣. He ruffs a club in hand and another heart in dummy. He ruffs another club in hand and the final heart in dummy. Now, he cashes Q♠, crosses back to hand with K♦ and draws the remaining trumps with ♠AK. Finally, he plays his A♦ and concedes the thirteenth trick to his opponents. Twelve tricks made.

This is a very straightforward version where, having cross-ruffed, declarer is still able to draw the opponents' trumps. When you use so many of your trumps for ruffing you will often not be able to draw your opponents' trumps later. So, before embarking on the cross-ruff, take your winners first in the suit which will not be involved in the cross-ruff. This is so that, while you merrily trump away, your opponents are not able to void themselves of that fourth suit and suddenly ruff your winning cards at the end.

Ruffing Losers in Dummy

Ruffing in dummy is usually a simple matter. Often, however, declarer is uncertain whether to ruff high or low. Generally, the rule should be to ruff low to begin with and high subsequently, when there is a greater chance of an opponent also being void in the suit. Naturally, if you can afford to ruff high from the outset, this you should do.

Hand 10   Dealer North

N	E	S	W
NB	NB	1S	NB
2S	NB	4S	

```
                    ♠ Q74
                    ♥ 102
                    ♦ 1086432
                    ♣ KJ
        ♠ A3        ┌─────────┐      ♠ 652
        ♥ J9765     │    N    │      ♥ Q4
        ♦ KJ        │ W     E │      ♦ A97
        ♣ 10987     │    S    │      ♣ 65432
                    └─────────┘
                    ♠ KJ1098
                    ♥ AK83
                    ♦ Q5
                    ♣ AQ
```

From a bleak selection, West leads 10♣ – top-of-a-sequence – and declarer assesses that he has a spade, two hearts and two diamonds to lose. To succeed, South must ruff two hearts in dummy and he must therefore delay drawing trumps. Winning

trick one in hand by overtaking J♣ with Q♣, declarer cashes
♥AK and then plays a third heart. To ruff low here would be
exceptionally careless. With all high trumps in hand (except the
ace), he can afford to ruff with 7♠, ensuring that, if East can
over-ruff, it will only be with the master trump. As it is, East is
void, but he cannot over-ruff. South returns to hand by overtaking K♣ with A♣ and ruffs his last heart with Q♠. Now, he can
draw trumps and fulfil his contract.

Had dummy's two lowest trumps been smaller still, South would
have had to risk ruffing low the first time and then, if successful,
use the queen for the second ruff when it was inevitable that one
opponent would be void.

Incidentally, perhaps West could have found the killing lead of
the ace and another trump – leaving only one trump in dummy
and South a heart ruff short for his contract. A simple raise by
responder may be based on 4-card support but, even playing
4-card majors, a simple raise can, and should, be made on 3-card
support with an outside shortage (a void, singleton or doubleton
in a side suit), since that shortage may be useful for ruffs. On
that basis, a trump lead may be right when a simple raise is
made. It certainly isn't a mandatory lead – something more
attacking, such as top-of-a-sequence will often be right – but
here a trump was certainly a possibility.

Many trump contracts will succeed simply by ensuring that you
make the required ruffs in dummy before drawing your opponents' trumps. However, obvious though this may be, there are
times when the methods you employ will prove crucial. Plan
your play here:

Hand 11   Dealer South

N	E	S	W	
–	–	2H†	NB	† *strong 2s*
2NT‡	NB	**4H**		‡ *something, but not much*

Hand 11   *Dealer South*

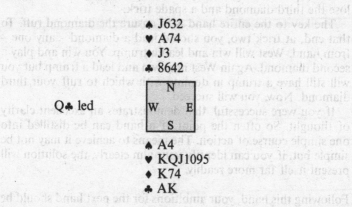

♠ J632
♥ A74
♦ J3
♣ 8642

Q♣ led

♠ A4
♥ KQJ1095
♦ K74
♣ AK

West leads Q♣ and you, declarer, assess that you hold a spade and three potential diamond losers. Assuming, as you should, that finesses will not succeed, plot your line of attack.

Hand 11
South in 4H

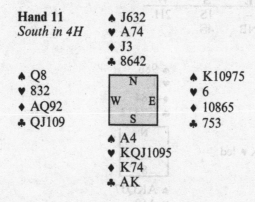

♠ J632
♥ A74
♦ J3
♣ 8642

♠ Q8
♥ 832
♦ AQ92
♣ QJ109

♠ K10975
♥ 6
♦ 10865
♣ 753

♠ A4
♥ KQJ1095
♦ K74
♣ AK

You won Q♣ with A♣. What did you lead at trick 2? Naturally, you resisted drawing trumps, but did you succumb to the temptation to cross to dummy's A♥ to lead a diamond towards your king? If you did, you will be beaten. West will win, note the diamond shortage in dummy and switch to a trump. You can concede another diamond but West will win again and play his last trump, denuding dummy of trumps. Now, you will have to lose the third diamond and a spade trick.

The key to the entire hand is to ensure the diamond ruff. To that end, at trick two, you should lead a diamond – any one – from hand. West will win and lead a trump. You win and play a second diamond. Again West may win and lead a trump but you will still have a trump in dummy with which to ruff your third diamond. Now, you will succeed.

If you were successful, that demonstrates an excellent clarity of thought. So often the point of a hand can be distilled into one simple course of action. The means to achieve it may not be simple but, if you can identify your aim clearly, the solution will present itself far more readily.

Following this hand, your ambitions for the next hand should be clear. Can you avoid the pitfalls and emerge successful?

Hand 12   Dealer South

N	E	S	W
–	–	1S	2H
2S	NB	4S	

```
              ♠ 986
              ♥ J2
              ♦ A84
              ♣ K7432
                  ┌───┐
                  │ N │
K♥ led          W │   │ E
                  │ S │
                  └───┘
              ♠ AKQJ7
              ♥ A53
              ♦ K52
              ♣ Q8
```

West leads K♥. What is your plan of attack and what action will you take during the early tricks?

Hand 12
South in 4S

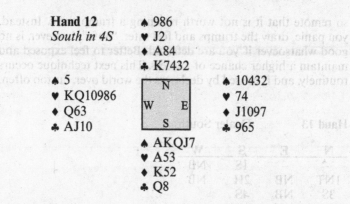

♠ 986
♥ J2
♦ A84
♣ K7432

♠ 5
♥ KQ10986
♦ Q63
♣ AJ10

♠ 10432
♥ 74
♦ J1097
♣ 965

♠ AKQJ7
♥ A53
♦ K52
♣ Q8

When the hand was first played, declarer ducked the first trick and won the continuation with A♥. He then cashed ♠AK and played his last heart and ruffed it in dummy. East over-ruffed and now South could not avoid losing a club and a diamond to go one off.

South does indeed hold four losers – two hearts, a diamond and a club – so a heart ruff seems the way to reduce these to three. However, West's overcall is crucial. Promising at least a 5-card suit, this should tip off declarer that East may be short in hearts and, with 10♠ outstanding, the danger of an over-ruff should be perceivable. The solution is to seek a ruff in dummy in a suit that is unlikely to split so poorly. To achieve this, you will require what I term a "loser exchange", a variation on the more usual "loser-on-loser" play, illustrated in hand 7 on page 27.

Declarer wins trick one with A♥ and returns a heart. West will win and, whether he switches – in which case declarer can win and play a third round of hearts – or whether West leads the third round of hearts himself, declarer should not ruff in dummy but instead discard a low diamond. Now, he is in control. If West foolishly persists in hearts, South can ruff or over-ruff East, regaining control. Whatever else West leads, declarer can win, cash ♦AK and ruff the third round of diamonds in dummy. Now, he can draw trumps and concede a club to West's A♣. The ruff in dummy has been achieved, but with far less risk of the over-ruff.

Sometimes you will feel that the chances of a ruff in dummy are so remote that it is not worth retaining a trump there. Instead, you panic, draw the trumps and feel safer. "Safe", however, is no good whatsoever if you are defeated. Better to feel exposed and maintain a higher chance of success. This next technique occurs routinely, and is missed by declarers the world over, far too often.

Hand 13   Dealer South

N	E	S	W
–	–	1S	NB
1NT	NB	2H	NB
3S	NB	4S	

```
                    ♠ K72
                    ♥ A53
                    ♦ J104
                    ♣ J753
      ♠ 85                        ♠ 963
      ♥ 87          N             ♥ J1094
      ♦ AKQ73   W       E         ♦ 98
      ♣ Q1096       S             ♣ K842
                    ♠ AQJ104
                    ♥ KQ62
                    ♦ 652
                    ♣ A
```

Once West has taken his ♦AKQ, South's only hope appears to be a 3–3 split in hearts. Is there an extra chance to add to the meagre 31.25% offered by a 3–3 split?

To succeed, South must be pragmatic: if the hearts do not split 3–3, it seems that he is defeated. However, if declarer were to leave one trump in dummy, he could test the heart suit and possibly still make a ruff in dummy if the hand with the heart shortage also held a trump shortage. Watch . . .

West takes the first three tricks with ♦AKQ and then, with neither a shortage nor a long suit in dummy, he switches to the safest thing he can think of: a trump. South wins in hand and

cashes a second round of trumps, preserving K♠ in dummy.
Now, before playing a third round of trumps, he plays K♥ and
A♥ and leads a third heart to his Q♥. If the hearts split 3–3,
South can draw the final trump and succeed; if, as it is in the
actual hand, West is out of hearts then, provided he holds no
more trumps, Q♥ holds the trick and South can ruff his fourth
heart in dummy with K♠. He can then return to hand with A♣
to draw the final trump from East's hand.

If the hearts are 3–3, declarer draws the final trump before enjoying his thirteenth heart. If the hearts are not 3–3 and the hand
which is short in hearts still holds the last trump, the hand cannot
be made. However, with this method, you have combined your
chances to furnish yourself with the greatest likelihood of success.

Ruffing in Dummy When There is No Shortage
Impossible, you might say, yet this is a technique that occurs
remarkably frequently. Since, very sensibly, you will be looking
for shortages when you want to ruff, it is important to be aware
that they are not necessarily necessary!

Hand 14   Dealer North

N	E	S	W
1NT†	NB	4S	

† *Strong NT opener (16–18pts)*

```
                  ♠ AJ4
                  ♥ A73
                  ♦ A92
                  ♣ AJ93
    ♠ 753          N           ♠ 9
    ♥ KQ95      W     E        ♥ 108
    ♦ QJ10                     ♦ K8743
    ♣ Q85          S           ♣ K10762
                  ♠ KQ10862
                  ♥ J642
                  ♦ 65
                  ♣ 4
```

West leads Q♦, and declarer faces three hearts and a diamond loser. There is no long suit in dummy which can be established and no shortages for ruffing, so must declarer rely on lucky breaks or defensive errors?

The key is that the definition of a "shortage" is any suit that is shorter in one hand than the other. Similarly, a "long suit" is one that is longer in one hand than the other.

Since dummy holds only three hearts and declarer four, there is a chance that a heart ruff can be achieved for declarer's tenth trick. Of course, trumps cannot be touched. Declarer wins the lead with dummy's A♦ and immediately plays A♥ and a low heart. West wins and, seeing that declarer is not drawing trumps, reasons that he may be seeking a ruff in dummy. To try to prevent this, West switches to a low trump. Declarer wins with J♠ in dummy and leads a third heart. Again West wins, and again the best that he can do is to play another trump. However, South is in control. He wins this trump trick in hand and plays his last heart, ruffing it in dummy with the ace of trumps – that can't be over-trumped. He can now cash A♣ and return to hand by ruffing a little club. He then draws West's last trump.

If dummy contains neither shortage nor long suit, ask yourself whether there is a suit longer in dummy than in your own hand which might provide a discard (this could well be a 3-card suit), or whether, when you hold more cards in a side suit in your hand than in dummy, there is any chance of a ruff, even if it takes four rounds of the suit to achieve it. These are all crucial plays which you may well have missed in the past, which will now improve your scores dramatically. But don't start playing until you have decided what you are going to try!

Ruffing in Hand

This is a technique beloved by bad bridge players. Generally, the trumps in your hand are for pulling your opponents' trumps; the trumps in dummy for ruffing your losers. You would not willingly wish to reduce the number of trumps in your hand, since often this will result in leaving one opponent with more trump length than you. Indeed, this is precisely the effect your opponents are attempting when they launch a forcing defence against you. At that point, you are likely to relinquish control of the hand to your opponents and fail.

You should only ruff in hand for one of four reasons:

1. You are being made to ruff by your opponents and either you have sufficient trump length that you can afford to ruff, or you have no other loser to discard (a "loser-on-loser" play – see page 27).

2. You are undertaking a cross-ruff, using each of your trumps separately.

3. You are establishing a long suit in dummy by ruffing out the high cards in your opponents' hands.

4. You can see that by making your low trumps separately, you can definitely accrue sufficient tricks to fulfil your contract.

Otherwise, try to resist the temptation to trump in your own hand.

Establishing Dummy's Long Suit

Quite simply, this is the most important section of this book. It is the third and last core method of creating extra tricks (or discarding losers).

Both in no-trumps and suit contracts, making the most of a long suit – usually in dummy – will be the key to success on the majority of bridge hands. From a defensive point of view, you will try to prevent the declarer from setting up that long suit, restricting his trick-taking potential.

In suit contracts, you have the advantage that your opponents' high cards can be trumped, allowing you to retain control of the play.

Let's start with a classic example. If any of this seems unclear, I urge you to lay out this deal in front of you and play it through. Once you are happy with this technique, your bridge scores will improve remarkably:

Hand 15   Dealer South

N	E	S	W
–	–	1C	NB
1H	NB	3C	NB
4C	NB	**5C**	

```
                    ♠ Q4
                    ♥ A8432
                    ♦ J4
                    ♣ Q972
        ♠ AJ52          N          ♠ K1083
        ♥ J7                       ♥ Q965
        ♦ Q9852     W     E        ♦ K1076
        ♣ 65            S          ♣ 3
                    ♠ 976
                    ♥ K10
                    ♦ A3
                    ♣ AKJ1084
```

West leads 5♦ and declarer realises that he has three spade losers and a diamond loser. There are plenty of trumps, so ruffing the third spade in dummy should be straightforward. However, there are no other shortages, so declarer still faces one loser too many. The solution will be to establish dummy's long heart suit and turn one of the low hearts into a winner, providing a discard for the losing 3♦.

Students often ask me if, by delaying drawing trumps, there isn't a risk that an opponent might ruff in and defeat the contract. The answer is yes, but since you have realised that you are a trick short for your contract, unless you try to make an extra trick, you will be defeated. When it appears that you hold too many losers (or not enough tricks) it is better to try to give yourself a chance of succeeding than to capitulate and give yourself no chance whatsoever. Indeed, the bonus for a game contract is so great that you can afford to fail by an extra trick many times over if, just once, your endeavours bring home a game contract.

So, South is going to try to make this contract and to this end he wins trick one with A♦ and immediately sets about establishing dummy's long suit. At trick two, South leads his K♥ and then 10♥ to dummy's ace. He now leads a low heart from dummy and ruffs it with a high trump in hand. This is both to prevent an over-ruff, but also to ensure that the trumps in dummy can be used as entries. If there is a prime thought to consider when you are trying to set up a long suit in dummy, it is this:

> *Preserve entries into the hand which contains the long suit you are trying to establish.*

This is vital since, not only will you need to reach that hand to play your long suit and make ruffs, but you will also need to reach the hand to enjoy the winners which you have sought so hard to establish.

South now draws a round of trumps by playing J♣ to dummy's Q♣ and he then plays another low heart and ruffs it with another high trump in hand. By now, neither opponent holds any more hearts, so the last one in dummy has been established into a winner. Declarer plays a low club to dummy's 9♣ – pulling out his opponents' last trump – and then plays his final low heart, on which he discards his losing 3♦.

That having been achieved, declarer can concede two spade tricks and then ruff the third round in dummy. 5C bid and made.

If this hand appears difficult, take the time to play the hand out, watching the effect of ruffing low cards in your own hand and thereby exhausting your opponents of their higher cards. Note also the importance of retaining entries into the dummy hand so that you can return to it to cash your hard-earned winner.

Suit Divisions
Incidentally, was it unlucky for South that the heart suit split 4–2? Wasn't it more likely that it would divide evenly? Top players know the percentage chances of all suit divisions and

they combine that information with any that they can discern from the auction, the opening lead and the general attitude of the defenders, in order to form a picture of their opponents' hands. That is all far too high-falutin' for us, but it is interesting to know the basic likelihoods of suit splits. And, here they are, in what I hope is an easy-to-remember format:

- If there is an even number of cards out against you, it is likely they will split oddly.
- If there is an odd number of cards out against you, it is likely that they will split as evenly as possible.

For example, if there are 6 cards out against you in your opponents' hands, they are unlikely to split 3–3; they are more likely to split 4–2; if there are 5 cards out against you, they are likely to split as evenly as possible, that is to say, 3–2.

Most commonly, as declarer, you hold seven, eight or nine trumps between your hand and dummy. The likely division of the outstanding cards, held by your opponents, should be important to you. Here are a few key percentages to illustrate the likely divisions:

With *nine* cards between you and your partner's hand:

- A 2–2 break of the outstanding 4 cards has a 37.5% chance, a 3–1 break 50% and a 4–0 break 12.5%.

With *eight* cards between you and your partner's hand:

- A 3–2 break has a 62.5% chance.

With *seven* cards between you and your partner's hand:

- A 3–3 break has only a 31.25% chance; a 4–2 break 46.88%.

As a result of these percentages, some players have become followers of an ancient creed to help them remember what to do in a suit headed by the ace-king-jack – but missing the queen:

"Eight Ever, Nine Never"

This is intended to suggest that with eight cards between you and your partner, missing the queen, you would always finesse for the queen; with nine cards between you, you would never finesse for the queen but instead cash ace and king and hope for the queen to fall under one of your top cards.

This is fine as far as it goes but, as your knowledge and expertise increases, you will find that, as usual, the rules you have been taught are only very basic guide-lines and there are plenty of logical, sensible times when they can be broken.

You may also be interested to know that the more poorly you shuffle the cards between deals, the more likely it is that cards will split evenly, since the cards tend to group into four of the same suit after a trick has been formed and will therefore be divided equally amongst the players. However, bad shuffling will also lead to dull, balanced hands which can prove very exhausting, and not a little dull, to everyone at the table. So shuffle up and shuffle well. To explode a well-known old-wives' tale: you cannot shuffle a deck too much!

Anyway, I must return to the most important card-play technique there is: suit establishment. This next hand cropped up in real life, but it looks like a text-book example, so here it is in a text-book. The declarer failed when it was first played. Would you?

Hand 16   Dealer South

N	E	S	W	
–	–	2C†	NB	† *game force*
2D‡	NB	2S	NB	‡ *relay*
3S	NB	4NT*	NB	* *Blackwood*
5D#	NB	6S	NB	# *one ace*

South's 2C was pushy and he continued to bid the hand aggressively, ending up in 6S.

Hand 16   *Dealer South*

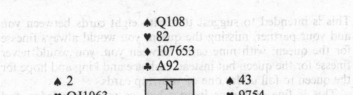

```
              ♠ Q108
              ♥ 82
              ♦ 107653
              ♣ A92
  ♠ 2                        ♠ 43
  ♥ QJ1063        N          ♥ 9754
  ♦ KJ2       W     E        ♦ AQ98
  ♣ Q865         S           ♣ 1073
              ♠ AKJ9765
              ♥ AK
              ♦ 4
              ♣ KJ4
```

West led Q♥ and declarer played the hand at lightning speed: he drew trumps, crossed to dummy with A♣ and took the club finesse. When West won with Q♣, the defence then took their A♦ to defeat the contract. Declarer claimed that he had no other chance, but he had ignored a declarer's greatest asset: a long suit in dummy. The diamonds may not look particularly salubrious, but their length is their strength and they can be established into the crucial extra trick which will allow declarer to spurn the club finesse.

South must plan to establish his diamonds and therefore preserve all means of entry into the dummy. He will have to delay drawing trumps, since they offer up to three entries to the dummy hand. South should win the lead with A♥ and play his 4♦ immediately. The opponents will take the trick, but South can win whatever is returned. Assuming it is another heart, declarer takes this and plays a low trump to dummy's Q♠ – drawing a round of trumps – and then he plays a low diamond and trumps it in hand with a high trump. He plays another low trump to dummy's 10♠ – drawing the final trump from East – and ruffs a low diamond in hand with a high trump. Again, he plays a low trump to dummy's 8♠ and ruffs another low diamond in hand. South can take particular satisfaction from this move, since it will draw out the last diamond from the opponents' hands – East's A♦! Finally, South can play a club to dummy's A♣ and then play the fifth and last diamond. This has been established into a winner, so South is able to discard his losing club and claim the rest of the tricks and his slam contract.

These hands are so vital that, again, if you are uncertain that you would be able to re-produce this play at the table, lay out the cards and play through the hand. I guarantee that by doing so, you will hugely improve your results, boost your confidence, and delight your partners.

The concept of suit establishment is, despite initial appearances, a relatively simple one: preserving your entries to the table, you go at dummy's long suit like a terrier with a rag – you never give up.

However, sometimes there are other concerns which will influence how you attack a long suit.

Hand 17   Dealer West

N	E	S	W
–	–	–	1C
NB	NB	2H†	NB
4H			

† *in the protective position, jump overcalls are strong*

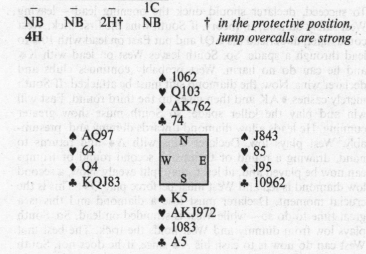

```
              ♠ 1062
              ♥ Q103
              ♦ AK762
              ♣ 74
 ♠ AQ97                    ♠ J843
 ♥ 64          N          ♥ 85
 ♦ Q4       W     E       ♦ J95
 ♣ KQJ83       S          ♣ 10962
              ♠ K5
              ♥ AKJ972
              ♦ 1083
              ♣ A5
```

West leads K♣ and South sees a diamond loser, a club loser and, since West is marked with A♠ from the auction, two spade losers. West is very likely to hold A♠ since there are only 16pts outstanding and West opened the bidding. How can declarer dispose of one of these losers?

Dummy contains a long diamond suit and, unless the remaining diamonds divide in an evil fashion, this will provide a discard for a spade loser. However, West's K♣ lead has exposed the club loser, a diamond will have to be conceded in order to set up the suit and, if East gains the lead, a spade will come winging its way through South's frail holding at double-quick time, leading to two further tricks for East-West. So, the challenge this time is to establish dummy's long suit whilst preventing East from gaining the lead. It is fine for West to have the lead, because he cannot lead a spade without giving you a trick, immediately or subsequently, with K♠. This type of play is known as "avoidance" – keeping one opponent off lead – and occurs more frequently in NT contracts (see page 109). However, there are many instances of avoidance being a vital winning technique at suit contracts also.

To succeed, declarer should duck the opening lead – leaving West safely on lead. In theory, if South wins the first trick, West could, later, underlead his ♣QJ and put East on lead with 10♣ to lead through a spade. So, South leaves West on lead with K♣ and he can do no harm. West probably continues clubs and declarer wins. Now, the diamond suit must be attacked. If South merely cashes ♦AK and then gives up the third round, East will win and play the killer spade; so South must show greater cunning. He leads a low diamond towards dummy and, presumably, West plays low. Declarer wins with A♦ and returns to hand, drawing a round of trumps. A second round of trumps can now be played and, at least, they split evenly. Now, a second low diamond is led and West must perforce play Q♦. This is the crucial moment. Declarer must lose a diamond and this is a great time to do so – while West is stranded on lead. So, South plays low from dummy and West holds the trick. The best that West can do now is to cash his A♠ since, if he does not, South will throw both spade losers away on his two winning diamonds.

What would happen if West played a second low diamond on the second round? South would have no choice but to win, and play a third round of diamonds, hoping that West held the final winning card. If East held ♦QJx, then South could not succeed.

This method played for West either to hold three diamonds or, if he only held one or two, to hold Q♦, at which point he could be forced to take the trick.

To solve a declarer problem such as this, it is necessary to realise that the diamond suit must be established. That having been accepted, you should then have time to analyse that to have East on lead threatens your spade holding, since West almost certainly holds A♠. From that point, you seek a solution. It is a matter of slow, logical steps, which is why as declarer you should take your time at trick one to assess the situation which faces you.

When dummy contains a 5- or 6-card suit, it is relatively easy to see the potential to establish that suit for discards. However, a long suit in dummy doesn't need to be long – merely **longer** than the holding in declarer's hand.

Hand 18   Dealer South

N	E	S	W	
–	–	2S†	NB	† *strong*
2NT‡	NB	4S		‡ *not much, but something*

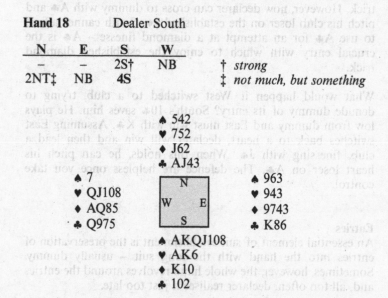

On Q♥ lead, declarer faces a heart, two diamonds and a club to lose. Dummy contains no shortages for ruffing and, apparently, no long suit. When the hand was first played, South drew trumps, crossed to A♣ in dummy and led a diamond. When West turned up with both honours, four tricks went to the opponents.

Despite appearances, there is a long suit in dummy – diamonds. It may look short and undistinguished to the uninitiated but, since it is longer than South's holding, there is potential for an extra trick, particularly since between them North-South hold three of the top five honours. Remembering the rule of preserving an entry to the hand with the long suit, A♣ must be preserved at all costs.

To succeed, declarer wins the lead with A♥, draws three rounds of trumps – he has no need of dummy's feeble offering – and then lays down K♦. West is likely to win and continue hearts. South wins and plays 10♦. If West does not take this, declarer is home, so we assume West wins and cashes his heart trick. However, now declarer can cross to dummy with A♣ and pitch his club loser on the established J♦. South cannot afford to use A♣ for an attempt at a diamond finesse – A♣ is the crucial entry with which to enjoy the established diamond trick.

What would happen if West switched to a club, trying to denude dummy of its entry? South's 10♣ saves him. He plays low from dummy and East must win with K♣. Assuming East switches back to a heart, declarer will win and then lead a club, finessing with J♣. When this holds, he can pitch his heart loser on A♣. The defence are helpless once you take control.

Entries

An essential element of suit establishment is the preservation of entries into the hand with the long suit – usually dummy. Sometimes, however, the whole hand revolves around the entries and, all too often, declarer realises it just too late.

Hand 19   Dealer South

N	E	S	W	
–	–	2H†	NB	† *strong*
2NT‡	NB	**4H**		‡ *not much, but something*

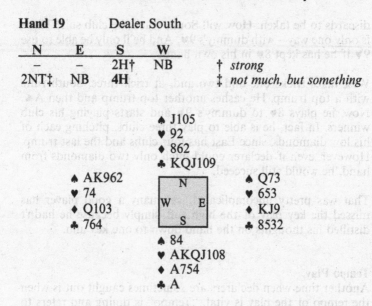

```
                    ♠ J105
                    ♥ 92
                    ♦ 862
                    ♣ KQJ109
    ♠ AK962                        ♠ Q73
    ♥ 74          ┌─────────┐      ♥ 653
    ♦ Q103        │    N    │      ♦ KJ9
    ♣ 764         │  W   E  │      ♣ 8532
                  │    S    │
                  └─────────┘
                    ♠ 84
                    ♥ AKQJ108
                    ♦ A754
                    ♣ A
```

West leads A♠ and, encouraged by East (see page 91), continues
with K♠ and 9♠, East playing his Q♠ at the third turn. Declarer
ruffs low, and settles down to make his plan. Too late – he is now
doomed to fail.

I have seen declarers play to the first trick even before dummy
has finished putting down his hand. I can't emphasize too much
how important it is to pause, once dummy appears, to form an
overview of the hand. Think about the bidding, the lead, assess
your winners or losers (or both) and, in a suit contract, select
which of the two core plays you are going to make: ruffing in
dummy or establishing a long suit. Even if your mind goes
blank, or you can't be bothered, at least give the impression of
making a plan – it will impress your partner and intimidate your
opponents.

Here, South faces two spade losers and three potential diamond
losers. Dummy contains a solid club suit, however, and, once
South has cashed A♣ – unblocking the suit – there are plenty of

discards to be taken. How will South reach the club suit? There is only one way – with dummy's 9♥. And he'll only be able to use 9♥ if he has kept 8♥ in his own hand.

West takes tricks one and two and, at trick three, South ruffs with a top trump. He cashes another top trump and then A♣. Now, he plays 8♥ to dummy's 9♥ and starts playing his club winners. In fact, he is able to play three clubs, pitching each of his low diamonds, since East has four clubs and the last trump. However, even if declarer could pitch only two diamonds from hand, he would still succeed.

That was pretty uncomplicated, yet many a good player has missed the key play of the high ruff simply because he hadn't distilled his thoughts on the hand down to one key aim.

Tempo Play
Another time when declarers are sometimes caught out is when the tempo of the play is vital. "Tempo" is timing and refers to the order in which you choose to play suits.
    For example, quite often you will find that you must take discards quickly, before your opponents can establish their own suit and cash their tricks.

Hand 20   Dealer South

N	E	S	W
–	–	1S	NB
3S	NB	4S	

West leads Q♣, and declarer sees that he has two trump losers, a heart and a club. There is no opportunity to make ruffs in dummy, so a long suit must be sought. Dummy's hearts are longer than declarer's so there is a potential discard there. Since declarer does not need the trumps in dummy either for ruffing or as entries, can he afford to draw trumps?

Hand 20   *Dealer South*

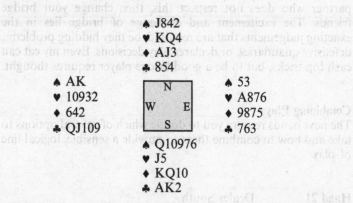

```
                    ♠ J842
                    ♥ KQ4
                    ♦ AJ3
                    ♣ 854
      ♠ AK           N          ♠ 53
      ♥ 10932                   ♥ A876
      ♦ 642       W    E        ♦ 9875
      ♣ QJ109        S          ♣ 763
                    ♠ Q10976
                    ♥ J5
                    ♦ KQ10
                    ♣ AK2
```

The answer is no. To see why, try to predict how the play will run.
Declarer takes the first trick and leads a trump. The defence will
win and continue with clubs. Declarer wins again and plays
another trump, which the defence will take. Now, they will cash
their winning club and wait to take A♥ to defeat the contract. The
timing – or, in bridge terms, the tempo – is off. To prevent the
defenders establishing a club trick for their side, declarer must
establish his own long suit before them and take his discard. To
that end, having won the first trick with A♣, declarer leads his J♥.
If this is ducked, he continues with 5♥ which East will certainly
win. East will return a club but, now, declarer can win with K♣,
cross to dummy with A♦ and play his winning heart, on which he
can discard his club loser. That having been achieved, he can then
draw trumps, and the defence will win only three tricks.

Take time to try to predict the likely play and check whether
your ideas have any chance of working. I suspect that every
declarer the world over has started play on a hand, knowing in
the back of his mind that his play has no chance of success. Why
do we do it? There is pressure from a glowering partner or
fidgeting opponents to hurry; there might be a feeling of wishing
that the hand were over and something easier might come along;
there might simply be a feeling that the hand cannot be made so
the best thing is to play badly and quickly. Resist these feelings,
strong though they may be. The tougher you find the hand, the

more time you require and, if you play with opponents and/or a
partner who does not respect this, then change your bridge
friends. The excitement and challenge of bridge lies in the
exacting judgements that are required: be they bidding problems,
defensive quandaries, or declarer play decisions. Even my cat can
cash top tricks, but to be a good bridge player requires thought.

Combining Plays

The next hands require you to decide which of several options to
take and how to combine them to provide a sensible, logical line
of play.

Hand 21   Dealer South

N	E	S	W
–	–	1H	NB
1NT	NB	4H	

Assess what is required here in order to provide the very best
chance of success.

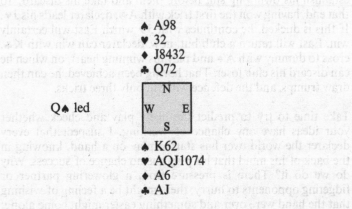

```
                    ♠ A98
                    ♥ 32
                    ♦ J8432
                    ♣ Q72
                         N
        Q♠ led       W       E
                         S
                    ♠ K62
                    ♥ AQJ1074
                    ♦ A6
                    ♣ AJ
```

Assuming, as you should, that finesses are failing, you have one
loser in each suit. There is no shortage in dummy, other than in

trumps, so ruffing is not an option. What about a long suit to establish? There are five diamonds which might be promising, but are there sufficient entries to set the suit up and then return to dummy to enjoy your winners? Sadly, no – only A♠ appears to be a means of access into the North hand. Is there another long suit to consider?

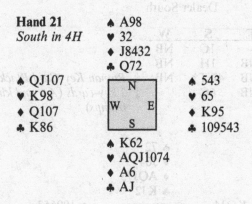

Hand 21
South in 4H

North:
♠ A98
♥ 32
♦ J8432
♣ Q72

West:
♠ QJ107
♥ K98
♦ Q107
♣ K86

East:
♠ 543
♥ 65
♦ K95
♣ 109543

South:
♠ K62
♥ AQJ1074
♦ A6
♣ AJ

There is – clubs. Not very long perhaps, but longer than in your own hand. Let's see how the play might run.

West leads Q♠ and your first decision is in which hand to win. If you were planning to take the trump finesse, or even the club finesse, you would win in dummy, but you don't need to hope that either will be right. There is a line offering close on 100% chance of success. Since you plan to establish an extra trick in dummy's "long" club suit, you preserve the entry into that hand, and choose to win in your own hand with K♠. Next, you lay down A♣ and J♣. Should West not win now, you have only three losers remaining, so you draw trumps quickly and claim your contract. Assuming that he does take his K♣, you can win whatever he leads next. Now, you can cross to dummy with A♠ and play your Q♣, pitching a loser (either a low spade or a low diamond). Since you are in dummy at this stage, you can now opt for a trump finesse if you choose. It loses, but nothing can stop you from making ten tricks now.

Hopefully, once you are clear in your own mind as to your aim on the hand, this seems quite simple. Yet, 90% of social bridge players would fail.

Next up, here is a tough slam to bring home.

Hand 22   Dealer South

N	E	S	W	
–	–	1C	NB	
1D	NB	1H	NB	
3C	NB	4NT†	NB	† *Roman Key-Card Blackwood*
5H‡	NB	**6C**		‡ *2 key-cards (A♦ and king of trumps)*

```
                    ♠ 72
                    ♥ J64
                    ♦ AQJ73
                    ♣ KJ2
   ♠ KQJ4          ┌─────┐          ♠ 109653
   ♥ 72            │  N  │          ♥ Q1095
   ♦ 10985       W │     │ E        ♦ K64
   ♣ 974           │  S  │          ♣ 8
                   └─────┘
                    ♠ A8
                    ♥ AK83
                    ♦ 2
                    ♣ AQ10653
```

West leads K♠ and you see that the hands are not fitting too well. There is a spade loser and two heart losers. There is no ruffing potential in dummy, but there is a long diamond suit. Should you take a finesse in diamonds or seek to establish the suit?

You have three certain entries to dummy: A♦ and ♣KJ, so it looks like you can set up the diamond suit, provided it splits reasonably. However, if you win trick one with A♠ and then take the diamond finesse, then should it lose, you will be defeated immediately. Generally, you would not take a finesse when you hold only one card in the opposite hand, since it may create a loser which wasn't there when you assessed the hand. The solution is to establish the diamond suit by taking what is known as a "ruffing finesse"; a technique which accelerates the establishment process and combines it with a "loser-on-loser" play.

South wins trick one with A♠ and delays drawing trumps, since dummy's cards are needed as outside entries. At trick two, South plays his diamond to A♦ and then returns Q♦ from dummy. If East covers with K♦, declarer ruffs, crosses to dummy by drawing a round of trumps to J♣ and then plays a low diamond and ruffs it high – to ensure it is not over-ruffed. Now, declarer can cash A♣ and draw the last trump by playing to K♣. J♦ fells West's 10♦ and 7♦ is a second winner. Both South's low hearts get discarded and the slam is home.

What happens if East does not cover Q♦ at trick three? Then, South should discard 8♠ from hand. As it is, Q♦ holds the trick and South can continue to play diamonds to establish the suit. If, however, West had won with K♦, then whatever he leads, South can regain the lead and continue to attack diamonds – dummy's J♦ is already a winner and a second winner can be established by ruffing. By pitching 8♠, even if West were to win, he could not cash a setting trick, and South keeps control.

If the hand seems tough – and it is – play the hand out by laying out the cards in front of you, and juggle the position of K♦ – you'll find wherever it is, you are at the helm and in control . . . And that's a nice feeling.

Combining plays is where declarer play gets tough, yet if you are confident about your suit establishment technique, then adding an additional element will not seem so hard in future.

Establishing a Second Suit in Hand

Before leaving the section on suit establishment – although the play will re-occur throughout this book – let's look at what happens when your establishable suit is in your own hand.

Hand 23   Dealer South

N	E	S	W
–	–	1D	NB
1S	NB	2C	NB
2D	NB	3C	NB
3D	NB	5D	

```
                   ♠ K7532
                   ♥ J765
                   ♦ K104
                   ♣ 6
    ♠ QJ10                      ♠ A984
    ♥ K1082         N           ♥ Q93
    ♦ 753        W     E        ♦ 92
    ♣ K98           S           ♣ J1074
                   ♠ 6
                   ♥ A4
                   ♦ AQJ86
                   ♣ AQ532
```

South has bid his hand several times over and, despite North's protestations of weakness, South has punted game. Dummy is better than it might have been, boasting three nice trumps. West might have led a trump, which would subsequently have embarrassed declarer but, as it is, on Q♠ lead, South may yet prevail.

Declarer played K♠ from dummy and East won with A♠, before switching to a low trump. Declarer ran this to dummy's K♦ and then led 6♣, finessing with his Q♣ when East played low. West won with K♣ and returned another trump, and now declarer couldn't establish his side suit. As Jill St. John in *Diamonds Are Forever* so winningly put it, "Too late! You had your chance, Curly, and you blew it!"

On Q♠ lead, declarer should realise that he has a loser in each major suit, and therefore his club suit must be established into winners. He will need to find the clubs dividing 4–3, and the king guarded by only two cards. This is about a one in three chance, but it is better than nothing.

Declarer loses the first trick and wins the trump switch in dummy with K♦. He plays a club to the ace in his hand and then a low club, ruffing in dummy. Returning to hand with A♥, he plays another low club and is delighted to see West produce the king. He ruffs that with dummy's last trump and ruffs another spade to return to hand. Now, he draws trumps, cashes Q♣ – felling East's J♣, and then enjoys his last club as his eleventh trick.

You need to be just as determined to establish your own side suit as you are when attacking dummy's long suit. As usual, when attacking a side suit, entries must be retained in the hand with the long suit, and trumps not drawn if they are required for ruffing, or as a means of access.

Advanced Plays – for hands with seemingly no hope:

This is an important little section, although the frequency of such hands is low, not because we don't all end up in hopeless contracts, but because usually ruffing in dummy or suit establishment will solve the problem. Here, however, we will glance at some more advanced solutions. The first example is so simple that when you find yourself in this situation this should become a standard procedure, even if you cannot imagine what might occur. You will be surprised how often good things happen as a result.

Simple Squeeze
Most social bridge players believe they have been squeezed when they throw away the wrong card, but that is not a squeeze, it is just bad play. A squeeze forces an opponent to throw away the wrong card; he is unable to protect two key cards in his hand as he has to discard something.

There are whole books on setting up squeezes, but they occur so infrequently and are so complicated to put into action, that there is really only one squeeze worth mentioning here – playing out all your trumps.

Hand 24   Dealer South

N	E	S	W	
	–	1S	NB	
2D	NB	3D	NB	
4NT†	NB	5C‡	NB	† *Roman Key-Card Blackwood*
6S				‡ *0 or 3 key cards*

♠ KQ3
♥ KJ104
♦ A1042
♣ Q9

♠ 104   ♠ 762
♥ 83   N   ♥ A9765
♦ Q83 W E ♦ J5
♣ KJ8764 S ♣ 1053

♠ AJ985
♥ Q2
♦ K976
♣ A2

Once South had agreed diamonds, North launched precipitously
into Roman Key-Card Blackwood and, upon hearing that South
held three key-cards (he hoped it wasn't none), he opted for a
slam in partner's first bid suit – spades. West led a low trump
and declarer assessed his chances.

South has a heart loser, a club loser and a diamond loser. One or
other of the minor suit losers can be pitched on dummy's long
heart suit, but it appears that ♦QJ will have to fall under the
ace-king for the contract to succeed. Declarer duly drew trumps
and then played a heart which pushed out A♥. East switched to
a club and South realised that he would not have led away from
K♣, so he rose with the ace and then cashed ♦AK. When Q♦
failed to fall, he conceded another trick for one down.

What would have happened if South had played out his trumps?
West would have come under terrible pressure. Trying to guard

both Q♦ and K♣ would have proved impossible and he would have had to part with one or the other. The squeeze would have bitten and declarer would have prevailed.

South draws trumps and pushes out A♥. He wins the club return with A♣ and cashes his two heart winners, pitching two low diamonds from hand. Now he returns to hand with K♦ and plays his fourth trump. No one is inconvenienced but, when South plays his last trump – the card that hurts you will often be the one that hurts your opponents more – West must try to protect both ♦Q8 and K♣, and he can't do it. If he pitches K♣, you throw away a diamond from dummy and your Q♣ is your twelfth trick; if he throws 8♦, you hope that the remaining diamonds are now splitting 1–1, and you discard your Q♣ from dummy. When you play your last diamond to A♦, the Q♦ and J♦ both fall and dummy's 10♦ is your twelfth trick. West cannot avoid giving you the contract.

Did you know that this is what would happen? You might have known but, even if unaware, by playing out your trumps you may squeeze an opponent or make him think he is being squeezed and force him to throw the wrong card (what experts call a "pseudo-squeeze"). Either way, don't give up, play out all your trumps and keep him guessing.

These are some simple rules to give yourself the best chance:

- To ensure that the squeeze bites effectively, you should have lost all the tricks you can afford to lose early on – this way, there will be no easy discards for your opponents to make.
- Ensure that you retain an entry into dummy if there is a chance that a card there may become a winner once the opponent has been forced to discard.
- Watch out for discomfort from your opponent, usually the one to play second to the final tricks. Such bottom-wriggling and brow-furrowing indicates that he is in difficulty and that is good news for you. The opponent who plays last has had a chance to watch your play and discards and may well be able to hang on to the right cards.

Elimination Endplay
When you started playing bridge a finesse must have seemed a really good deal – a 50% chance of making a trick with a low card. As a more experienced player, 50% should seem a bad deal, especially if you could create a certainty.

Wouldn't it be nice if, instead of having to finesse, your opponents led the suit around to you, allowing you to win cheaply or capture their honour card? Your opponents will not willingly co-operate, so you must compel them, by eliminating all the safe ways for them to get off lead, so that they have to lead what you want them to play, or face the consequences.

Hand 25   **Dealer South**

N	E	S	W	
–	–	2S†	NB	† *strong*
4S‡	NB	6S		‡ *good support, no aces*

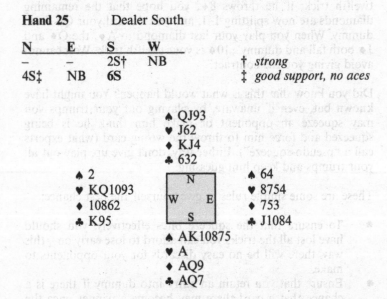

♠ QJ93
♥ J62
♦ KJ4
♣ 632

♠ 2
♥ KQ1093
♦ 10862
♣ K95

♠ 64
♥ 8754
♦ 753
♣ J1084

♠ AK10875
♥ A
♦ AQ9
♣ AQ7

West leads K♥ against South's slam, and declarer soon realises that his fate depends on the position of the club suit. Unfortunately, when he takes the club finesse by leading from dummy towards his Q♣, it loses to West's K♣. Later, East makes his J♣ and the contract is defeated. If only declarer could have persuaded West to lead a club . . .

As you can see, West would not want to lead a club away from his king, so South must make leading anything else either impossible, or deeply unpalatable. This is what he does.

South wins K♥ lead with A♥ and draws two rounds of trumps, ending in dummy. Now, he plays 6♥ and trumps it in his own hand. Next he plays all three rounds of diamonds, ending in dummy. Finally, knowing from the lead that West holds Q♥, he plays J♥ and discards his losing 7♣ on it. This is a "loser-on-loser" play. The effect is that West must win with Q♥ or squander the trick. Now, what can West lead? He cannot play trumps – they have gone; he cannot play a diamond or another heart because, if he does, declarer can trump in dummy, and discard the losing Q♣ from hand – a so-called "ruff and discard". West will know this and will reason that the only suit to give him any chance of not providing you with a trick is a club and, when he leads that, you have made your contract.

If you find this a difficult concept – and it is – lay out the cards and play out the hand to see the effect. Years ago, I spent a month in bed, very unwell, reading a thick, detailed tome on endplays. The first hand I played when I was better – and I mean the first – was an endplay hand and I missed it. It almost caused a relapse I was so ashamed of myself.

Let's look at it in some more detail. To plan a successful elimination endplay, you must ensure that there are trumps left in both your hand and dummy – this is so that, if your opponent leads a suit in which you have no cards left in either hand, you are able to ruff in one hand and discard a loser from the other.

Next, you must eliminate the side suits, so that there are no cards left in either your hand or dummy. Notice that you achieved this on this hand by trumping a low heart in hand early on, then playing out all your diamonds – so that West could not lead one when he gained the lead – and then, finally, playing your last heart and pitching the club you were always going to lose onto it, so that West had to win the trick.

Finally, you must exit (get off lead), so that your opponent is forced to lead what you want. A "loser-on-loser" play often achieves this aim.

Let's see one further declarer play example in this section:

Hand 26   Dealer South

N	E	S	W	
–	–	1C	NB	
3C	NB	3D†	NB	† *cue-bids, showing first round*
3S†	NB	6C		*control in these suits*

```
                  ♠ AK
                  ♥ 753
                  ♦ K97
                  ♣ J10642
   ♠ 10752          N          ♠ QJ963
   ♥ KJ6                       ♥ 9842
   ♦ J1085      W     E        ♦ 432
   ♣ Q5            S           ♣ 7
                  ♠ 84
                  ♥ AQ10
                  ♦ AQ6
                  ♣ AK983
```

West leads J♦ against South's slam. Assuming that the trumps break 2–1, declarer has no worries except in hearts where he could take a double finesse, hoping that East held either J♥ or K♥. As it is, both finesses would fail and South would be defeated. Let's plan the play to ensure that West helps us to make the contract.

South wins the lead in his hand with Q♦ and draws two rounds of trumps. Before he takes the first heart finesse, he wants to ensure that West cannot get off lead again safely should he win the trick. To this end, declarer plays out his other two diamonds and then cashes ♠AK, leaving voids in both suits in both hands. Now, he plays a low heart from dummy and finesses (it doesn't matter if he plays his Q♥ or his 10♥) and West takes the trick. However, West has no escape: if he plays a spade or a diamond, declarer can trump in dummy and throw away his other low heart. If West leads a heart, South runs it around to his hand and wins both the heart tricks. Contract made 100% of the time.

Counting

One of the biggest steps a player can take is moving from worrying about just his own hand and dummy, to thinking about the entire deal. Trying to picture all four hands is, on most hands, remarkably difficult but, if you make the effort, you will find that more and more times you are able to form a coherent idea of your opponents' cards. If one or both opponents have bid, you have both point-count and distributional information from which to work. Even if they have been silent, you may be able to draw important deductions from their lack of action. In this section, some of the expert techniques for locating opponents' cards are revealed. For me, this is one of the most exciting parts of the game – the detective work: the facts you know, the inferences you can take, the deductions that you draw.

Most importantly, when you are trying to form a picture of all four hands, do not concern yourself with what your opponents have left in their hands. Think about their initial hand pattern (shape of hand) and point-counts because, otherwise, you will be dealing with images that change after every trick.

Finally, if your opponents have bid during the auction and you end up as declarer, you have a substantial advantage. As part of forming your overview of the hand, assess how many points the bidding opponent is likely to be marked with – you may well find that your other opponent has almost nothing – and then you will be able to place outstanding high cards with ease.

Hand 27   Dealer West

N	E	S	W	
–	–	–	1NT†	† *Weak NT (12–14pts)*
NB	NB	Dbl	NB	
NB	2C	4H		

Hand 27   *Dealer West*

```
              ♠ 9642
              ♥ 52
              ♦ A1032
              ♣ 864
  ♠ AKQ10      ┌─────┐      ♠ J83
  ♥ 943        │  N  │      ♥ J7
  ♦ 987      W │     │ E    ♦ Q65
  ♣ A103       │  S  │      ♣ J9752
              └─────┘
              ♠ 75
              ♥ AKQ1086
              ♦ KJ4
              ♣ KQ
```

South first looks for a big penalty double of West's weak 1NT but, when East rescues his partner into clubs, South decides to have a punt at game.

West leads A♠ and declarer assesses the situation. He has two spades and a club to lose and a two-way finesse in diamonds. If he believes West holds Q♦, he can lead a low diamond and finesse with dummy's 10♦; if he thinks East holds Q♦, he can lead a diamond from dummy and, when East plays low, put in J♦ from hand.

A key element of successful declarer play is that, when a suit offers you a two-way finesse, you should delay taking it until the last possible moment. In this way, you can accrue as much information as possible about the position of the missing honour card.

Here, South holds 18pts and dummy 4pts, making a total of 22pts. This leaves 18pts for the opponents, of which, from the auction, West holds 12–14pts. East is therefore marked with 4–6pts. If declarer had to make a decision about the position of Q♦ now, he would probably play West to hold it, since he started with many more points than East. However, there is no hurry. The entire hand revolves around locating Q♦ and that is what South must concentrate upon.

West has led A♠ and follows with K♠ and then Q♠ which South ruffs. Not requiring dummy's trumps for any purpose, he draws out the opponents' trumps in three rounds and now plays a club. When West wins with A♣ and leads a fourth round of spades, declarer can relax – he knows who holds Q♦. West has shown up with ♠AKQ – that is 9pts – and A♣ – a further 4pts, making a total of 13pts. He cannot hold Q♦ also, since that would give him 15pts and he would not have opened 1NT.

Declarer ruffs the spade, plays a diamond to the ace and then leads a low diamond, playing J♦ from hand when East plays low. This holds and the contract is made. There is no excuse for a thoughtful player to fail here, yet it happens all the time.

Playing for the impossible is easily done, especially in the heat of battle. Simple counting techniques will help you to banish hopeless lines in favour of those with a chance.

Hand 28   **Dealer West**

N	E	S	W
–	–	–	1S
Dbl	2S†	4H	

† *very weak*

♠ A3
♥ KJ73
♦ K543
♣ J105

♠ KQ10962
♥ 42
♦ Q6
♣ A93

♠ 874
♥ A6
♦ 10982
♣ 7642

♠ J5
♥ Q10985
♦ AJ7
♣ KQ8

When this hand was first played, South won the opening K♠ lead and started pulling trumps. When East took A♥ and returned a spade, West won and then got off lead with another trump. Declarer took the diamond finesse, which lost to West's Q♦; West then cashed A♣ to defeat the contract. South's line of play had been a hopeless one as he had failed to corral the facts to form a coherent, logical plan.

On K♠ lead, declarer assesses that he holds a loser in every suit. He and dummy hold a total of 25pts between them, leaving 15pts for his opponents, most of which must be held by West, who opened the bidding. When he discovers that East holds A♥, this leaves only 11pts, so he knows for certain that Q♦ is in the West hand. The finesse into West now becomes a hopeless play.

Since South does not hold ♦109, he cannot finesse against West for the queen since, if he leads J♦, West will cover and East's 10♦ will be promoted into the setting trick. Having drawn trumps and pushed out A♣, the only play to offer any chance of success is to cash ♦AK and hope that Q♦ drops. Since West is likely to hold five or six spades for his 11pt opening bid and has shown up with two trumps and at least three clubs by now, a doubleton diamond is quite possible. Q♦ does indeed fall and the game contract is made.

Incidentally, it is worth playing all the other suits out first since it is possible that the defence will go wrong and either player might lead a third spade – giving you a ruff and discard – or West may lead a diamond around to you: it's unlikely, but possible.

If the hand were slightly different, you would have an alternative play – and a very pretty one it is too:

Hand 29   Dealer West

N	E	S	W
–	–	–	1S
Dbl	2S†	4H	

† *very weak*

Hand 29   *Dealer West*

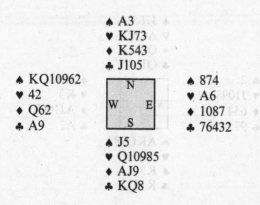

♠ A3
♥ KJ73
♦ K543
♣ J105

♠ KQ10962
♥ 42
♦ Q62
♣ A9

♠ 874
♥ A6
♦ 1087
♣ 76432

♠ J5
♥ Q10985
♦ AJ9
♣ KQ8

The auction is identical, but South now holds 9♦ instead of a smaller one. When declarer plays out trumps and clubs, he notes that West holds only two cards in each suit. It is almost certain therefore that he holds at least three diamonds so, now, playing for the drop has no chance. Since South is still certain that West holds Q♦, he knows that the finesse will fail, but East could easily hold 10♦ and, if that is so, there is a finesse available through him. So, South plays the diamonds in the following unconventional fashion:

He leads J♦ from hand and West covers with Q♦ (if West does not, South runs J♦ and expects it to win the trick). South beats West's Q♦ with dummy's K♦. Now, he leads a low diamond from dummy and, when East plays low, he finesses against 10♦ by putting in his 9♦. This duly holds the trick and the contract is again made. If West held ♦Q10x then, assuming correct defence, the contract cannot be made.

Hand 30   Dealer East

N	E	S	W
–	1D	1S	NB
3S	NB	4S	

Hand 30   *Dealer East*

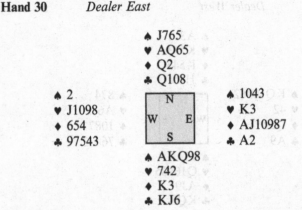

```
               ♠ J765
               ♥ AQ65
               ♦ Q2
               ♣ Q108
 ♠ 2          ┌─────────┐    ♠ 1043
 ♥ J1098      │    N    │    ♥ K3
 ♦ 654        │ W     E │    ♦ AJ10987
 ♣ 97543      │    S    │    ♣ A2
              └─────────┘
               ♠ AKQ98
               ♥ 742
               ♦ K3
               ♣ KJ6
```

West leads 5♦ (MUD – see page 146) and declarer sees that he
has two minor suit aces to lose and two potential heart losers. A
count of the total points reveals that the declarer's side holds
27pts; the defence 13pts. Since East opened the bidding, it is
close on certain that he holds K♥. Clearly, there can be no point
in taking the heart finesse into East's hand. Having drawn
trumps and pushed out A♣, South should play out the minor
suits. He discovers that East holds three trumps, two clubs and
five or six diamonds. This makes the possibility of a doubleton
heart in East's hand very real and the correct line in hearts is now
to play A♥ and a low one, hoping K♥ must be played on the
second round. It is, and dummy's Q♥ is the tenth trick.

Once you focus on the fact that the Q♥ is your only hope of
an extra trick, the count reveals that the finesse is redundant,
and the play of A♥ and a low one becomes obvious.

Incidentally, when playing a weak NT, to open 1NT with hands
containing a 5-card minor suit is standard, so those hands with
12–14pts which are opened with 1C or 1D often contain six card
suits. This makes a doubleton heart on this hand even more
likely.

When I played this next hand, many years ago, I came to my
senses only just in time. The opponents' bidding is less revealing,
but a key deduction can still be made:

Hand 31   Dealer South

N	E	S	W
–	–	1H	NB
3H†	NB	**4H**	

† *limit raise (10–12pts;*
  4-card spade support)

♠ Q96
♥ A873
♦ KQ84
♣ 97

A♠ led

```
    N
  W   E
    S
```

♠ J107
♥ QJ1062
♦ AJ3
♣ AQ

West led A♠. I assessed that I had two spades and a trump to lose. However, East encouraged the lead and West continued with K♠ and a third spade, which East ruffed, before exiting safely with a diamond. Does my game contract now rely upon the trump finesse?

Disheartened, I led Q♥ and West smoothly played low. I was about to play low from dummy too when my opponents' bidding came back to haunt me . . . There had been no bidding! I was surprised that West had failed to overcall with a five-card spade suit headed by ace-king but I was certain that if he had also held K♥, he would have bid. This realisation meant that to take the heart finesse would be madness. My only hope – since I was certain that East held that card – was that it was now a singleton. So, I called for A♥ from dummy and held my breath. East angrily slapped K♥ on the table and glared at me as if I had seen his hand. I certainly hadn't, but drawing the correct deduction from the auction – or lack of it – was just as good as leaning over and picking through East's cards. It was a clear case of the dog that did not bark in the night.

Hand 31
South in 4H

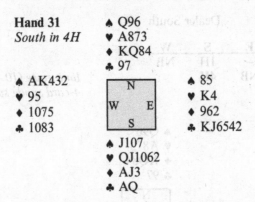

♠ Q96
♥ A873
♦ KQ84
♣ 97

♠ AK432
♥ 95
♦ 1075
♣ 1083

♠ 85
♥ K4
♦ 962
♣ KJ6542

♠ J107
♥ QJ1062
♦ AJ3
♣ AQ

There will be more counting hands in the NT Play section, starting on page 103, and these will include a count of the distribution which does not necessarily require the opponents to have bid. However, from now on, whenever your opponents do bid, take time to add up the total points for your side and calculate your opponents' points. You will be surprised how many problems it solves, even at trick one.

As well as points, there are deductions to be drawn from what your opponent leads and what he fails to lead, particularly if he chooses a suit which, to you, seems peculiar. Either your opponent is peculiar – which is more common than you might think – or something is amiss. It's up to you to work out which and what!

Hand 32   Dealer North

N	E	S	W
1D	1H	1S	2H
2S	NB	4S	

It is often a good idea to try to anticipate what your opponent might lead. Then, if he opts for something different, you'll be alerted. What do you expect West to lead here?

Presumably, a heart. His side has bid and agreed the suit. However, if West does not lead a heart, it could be because he holds the ace and does not want to risk leading away from it (see page 84). The suit you would least expect West to lead is diamonds, because to lead dummy's long suit is usually madness. On this deal, West leads 7♦! What does that mean, and how will it affect your play?

Hand 32   *Dealer North*

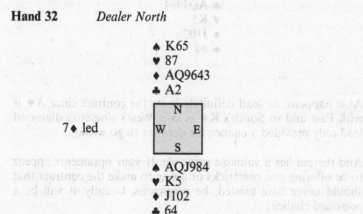

♠ K65
♥ 87
♦ AQ9643
♣ A2

7♦ led

♠ AQJ984
♥ K5
♦ J102
♣ 64

South counts his losers: none in trumps, two potential losers in hearts, one in diamonds and one in clubs. However, dummy's long diamond suit will provide discards and, at the very least, it will be possible to pitch one losing club from hand. Once trumps are drawn all should be well. Indeed, if West had led from K♦, declarer may make all thirteen tricks. So, should South play low from dummy at trick one?

Definitely not! The only rational explanation for West's lead is that it is a singleton and that he hopes that East will win K♦, provide a ruff in diamonds and then put East back on lead with A♥ for another diamond ruff. That would be the first four tricks to the defence. South should rise with dummy's A♦, pull trumps, and give up K♦ to East. Even if East-West take two heart tricks, declarer still holds A♣. He can win that card and then get over to dummy to pitch his club loser from hand on a winning diamond. The full deal looked like this:

Hand 32
South in 4S

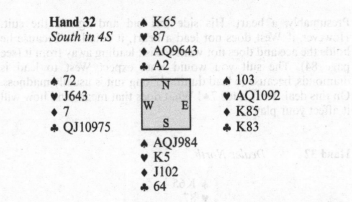

♠ K65
♥ 87
♦ AQ9643
♣ A2

♠ 72   ♠ 103
♥ J643   ♥ AQ1092
♦ 7   ♦ K85
♣ QJ10975   ♣ K83

♠ AQJ984
♥ K5
♦ J102
♣ 64

As it happens, no lead definitely beats the contract since A♥ is with East and so South's K♥ is safe. West's singleton diamond lead only provided a chance for declarer to go wrong.

And therein lies a valuable principle. If your opponents appear to be offering you overtricks or a way to make the contract that should never have existed, be suspicious. Usually, it will be a poisoned chalice . . .

Safety Play
Finally, a technique which is applicable to both suit and no-trump contracts. When you are in the luxurious position of being able to see your contract for the taking, instead of relaxing, use the time to ask yourself what might go wrong. The most likely disaster to strike unwary declarers is when a suit splits badly, particularly the trump suit. There are numerous Safety Plays to guard against the loss of too many tricks should a suit behave badly and whole books have been written on the subject. Here, however, we will look at just one: the one that crops up most often.

The principle of a Safety Play is to be prepared to squander a possible overtrick to ensure that you make your contract. Duplicate players, for whom overtricks can be crucial, often have to spurn such tactics but, for rubber bridge or Chicago players, as well as competitors in Teams of Four matches, safeguarding your contract is paramount. This everyday example does not even risk your overtrick – it is the perfect safety play.

Hand 33   Dealer South

N	E	S	W
–	–	1H	NB
3H	NB	4H	

♠ 65
♥ K753
♦ 102
♣ KQJ84

♠ J742   ♠ Q103
♥ 9   ♥ QJ42
♦ AKJ43   ♦ Q965
♣ 652   ♣ 103

♠ AK98
♥ A1086
♦ 87
♣ A97

West leads A♦ and South assesses his position. He has two diamonds and two spades to lose and a trump loser. However, his spade losers can be thrown away on dummy's long club suit so, really, he seems to have only three losers about which to worry. If South gives no further thought to the hand, West will play ♦AK and then switch and declarer will gain the lead at trick three. He will play his ♥AK and discover the bad news – East started with four trumps and must now make two of them. South will go at least one down.

This most common scenario can be dealt with to the declarer's satisfaction, if he is alert. For example, when he holds eight cards in a suit, headed by ace, king and ten, he can guard against one of his opponents holding four trumps headed by queen-jack.

When declarer plays his hearts, he leads 6♥ to dummy's king, preserving the top honour that is in the same hand as the ten. Now, he leads a low heart from dummy and, if East plays small, he puts in the 10♥ from his hand. If West now wins with an honour, there is only one heart outstanding and it will fall under A♥ when South plays it later. If, instead, as happens here, West shows out, South can now start playing on clubs until East trumps in once, and then he can draw East's last trump with his A♥ and enjoy the rest of the clubs.

Even if East puts in the queen or jack when a low heart is first led from dummy, South is in control. He can beat that honour with his A♥, cross to dummy's K♣ with a low club from hand, and lead another trump through East's hand, ensuring that he scores his 10♥ and only loses one trick in hearts.

If West had held the four trumps, South would have been helpless, because dummy does not contain the ten sitting over West. But, if a contract really can't be made, it is comforting to think that you did your very best.

By the way, even if the ace, king and ten start off all in the same hand, the safety play can still be made:

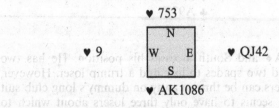

In this example, South would cash A♥ from hand and then cross to dummy in a different suit. Then he would lead a low heart from dummy and, if East plays low – which, to keep declarer guessing, he usually should – South can insert 10♥ as before.

Deceptive Carding – with which card to win?
It may not seem important but, when you have a choice of cards with which you can win a trick, it will help to keep your opponents guessing if you win with the correct card. Here is a

brief guide to the most common – and revealing – positions.

You are playing in a contract of 4S and your opponent leads a heart. With which card should you win?

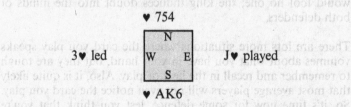

♥ 754

3♥ led   J♥ played

♥ AK6

The correct card to play is the ace. This is because East knows that his partner would not lead away from an ace against a suit contract (see page 84) and West knows that as East has not won the trick with the ace, declarer must have it. You are, therefore, winning with the card both defenders know that you hold. However, either defender may hold the king and their partner will be kept guessing. If you win with king, each of them will know that you also hold the ace and you'll be fooling no one.

This time, you are playing in 3NT and the layout is exactly the same. Assuming that you decide not to hold up (see page 105), with which card should you win now?

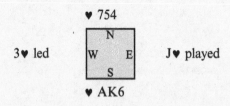

♥ 754

3♥ led   J♥ played

♥ AK6

You should win with the king! This is because, had you held ♥Axx, you would not have won the first trick at all – you would definitely have held up (see page 105). For that reason, each defender will know that you also hold the king. If, on the other hand, you take this trick with the king, it is quite possible that

West has led away from the ace (since this is allowed against NT contracts) and you dare not duck because East will lead the suit back through your hand. Similarly, although unlikely, West may think that East could hold the ace and he has withheld it on the first round for reasons of entry preservation. Either way, the ace would fool no one; the king induces doubt into the minds of both defenders.

There are lots more situations where the card you play speaks volumes about what you have in your hand, but they are tough to remember and recall in the heat of play. Also, it is quite likely that most average players will not even notice the card you play. So, it's time now for some defence, lest you think that you're about to make every contract you ever bid!

3

SUIT CONTRACTS – FOCUS ON DEFENCE

Your basic strategy for defending suit contracts should be to assess the likely tactics of the declarer and then seek to foil them at every opportunity. We have already seen that the auction can sometimes reveal, in advance of your opening lead, what style of hand may be about to occur but, frequently, it is not too late to adjust once you have had the luxury of seeing dummy.

To begin, let's take a look at the problems of finding a good opening lead and whether that lead should be attacking and risky or passive and safe.

Lead Styles

As a general rule, the more confident your opponents and their auction sounds, the more aggressive you should be with your lead. After all, if it looks like they are going to make their contract, then only something pretty exciting is likely to stop them. Even if you give away an overtrick from time to time, it will be worth it to beat a few game contracts. (This may well not be true at duplicate, where overtricks are so valuable and, hence, tactics change.) Conversely, if your opponents' auction sounds strained and they appear to have stretched to game or have been pushed by your own competitive bidding, then a safe, passive lead which does not risk giving anything away will be called for.

For the sake of simplicity, let's assume that all leads are either aggressive or passive (although there is space in between) so that you have a good idea of what to choose once you have decided upon your style of action.

Let's look at some general thoughts and then study the detail.

Aggressive Leads

These involve an element of risk. For example, if you lead a low card from a suit headed by an honour, that honour card is no longer involved in the trick and your opponents may be able to win the trick using a lower card.

Doubletons

Leading from a doubleton is one of the all-time favourite leads of bridge players. It is so aggressive that it almost always results in providing declarer with an extra trick. Even leading from an ace and a low card is incredibly dangerous. Make your rule: NEVER lead a doubleton against a suit contract, unless your partner has called the suit.

This also has the huge benefit of reducing your partner's angst when you lead from a suit in which partner can deduce you must be short. Instead of agonizing over whether you have led a singleton or a doubleton, he will know that it is a singleton.

Singletons

To lead a singleton is still aggressive, since it may well be your opponents' longest side suit. At least if partner does hold the ace, you will be able to score a ruff immediately and that may be enough to defeat the contract. However, to lead a singleton in a suit that has been bid by your opponents is asking for trouble, unless you have strong reason to believe that your partner may hold the ace.

Whenever you lead from a shortage, to achieve success your partner must win and return the suit to give you a ruff before the declarer has drawn your trumps. Therefore, the weaker you are, the more attractive a singleton lead will become; the stronger you are, the less chance there is of partner holding entries and the less attractive a singleton lead becomes.

Leading a small card (lowest from three; fourth highest) from a
suit headed by a king
Leading away from a suit headed by a king is an aggressive move
because the declarer or dummy may be able to win the trick
cheaply with the queen. However, it is often essential to set up
tricks for your side quickly, before declarer can pitch his losers.

Do not lead a suit which is headed by an ace. Why not? Let's
take a look at just one suit to see the effect. South, the declarer,
is playing with spades as trumps and you, as West, have decided
to lead a low heart away from your A♥:

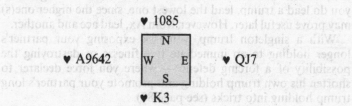

♥ 1085

♥ A9642   W   E   ♥ QJ7

♥ K3

You lead 4♥ and this runs to East's J♥ and declarer's K♥. This
is a trick declarer could never have made. If you had not led a
heart but waited for dummy, declarer or your partner to lead a
heart, your A♥ always beats declarer's K♥.

The same thing occurs if you lead A♥ – the king is established
for South.

Even worse, declarer may hold a singleton K♥ then, not only
will K♥ make, but your A♥ will get trumped when you try to
play it later.

So, don't do it! Never lead a suit headed by the ace against a
suit contract unless it is your partner's suit, it is the trump suit,
or if you also hold the king. To lead the ace from ace-king is
quite acceptable as it allows you to see dummy and your
partner's reaction to your lead (see page 105) without taking too
great a risk of squandering tricks.

Passive Leads
These are those which are either very safe or offer less chance of
actively taking tricks. However, as illustrated in Chapter 1,
whenever dummy is relatively balanced, declarer will struggle to
make his tricks. In these situations contracts can often be beaten

simply by not providing the declarer with free tricks. For this reason, unless the auction warns the defence of a long, strong suit in dummy, the opening lead should usually be a passive one.

Leading Trumps

This should be done when holding a small doubleton (perhaps Ax) or three trumps provided that, by leading trumps, you do not sacrifice a trump trick of your own. Leading from Qxx for example will probably allow declarer to win the first trick cheaply with the jack and then fell your queen under the ace and king. When you do lead a trump, lead the lowest one, since the higher one(s) may prove useful later. However, from Ax, lead ace and another.

With a singleton trump, you risk exposing your partner's longer holding to an immediate free finesse or destroying the possibility of a forcing defence – where you force declarer to shorten his own trump holding and promote your partner's long trump holding into tricks (see page 87).

When you yourself hold four trumps, leading your own long suit in an attempt to make declarer ruff and shorten his own holding will generally prove more profitable.

Top-of-a-Sequence

These leads are generally very safe, since they push out the missing higher cards and promote your own holding into tricks, without risking giving away any tricks in the process. High sequences, such as suits headed by ace-king or king-queen are particularly effective. There are also top-of-internal-sequences. The detail on all these leads follows this section.

Leading small cards (lowest from three; fourth highest) from suits headed by queen (or jack-ten)

These leads offer some chance of trick establishment while taking a small risk. If partner holds a touching honour, the lead is likely to work well.

Top-of-Rubbish

Leading a high intermediate card (the intermediates are 2–9) indicates a lack of interest in the suit you are leading. This is a rotten lead (although better than leading from an ace or from a doubleton in an unbid suit, or even leading a trump when you need somehow to attack) since it is from weakness, provides only a negative angle for your partner, and risks exposing him to finesses. However, as all bridge players know, in real life there is no such thing as an easy lead and, if all you have are revolting choices, your duty is to pick the least revolting and it may just turn out that this is it.

General Policy for Opening Leads Against Suit Contracts
Since the vast majority of good defence against suit contracts is about not giving away tricks, you will most often select a passive lead unless the auction suggests otherwise. This is why it is so important to form an opinion of the auction before leading. The three key styles of declarer play will involve ruffing in dummy, establishing a long suit in dummy, or relying on finesses and mis-defences. If you can identify which auction you have just heard, you can then choose your style of lead to fit the task.

In the examples of defensive play, challenge yourself to find the correct style of opening lead and, if possible, the correct card.

Take this hand and imagine that you are on lead three times, against three different auctions. Analyse the auction, decide what plan the declarer may have and then seek to counter it with your opening lead:

West		a) North	South
♠ KJ72		–	1H
♥ 863		2H	3H
♦ J1095		**4H**	
♣ A3			
		b) 1C	1H
		2C	3H
		4H	
		c) –	1H
		2NT	**4H**

Virtually any lead may turn out to be correct, but the recommended one will work more often than the others:

a)   North-South have edged their way gingerly into game; since they offer such enticing bonuses, game contracts are likely to be bid if there is the sniff of success. If they are short of high-card points, they will be relying upon ruffs to make their contract. A trump lead is called for to cut down this potential straight away. Lead your lowest trump: 3♥.

b)   Here, the bidding reveals that dummy will hold a long club suit on which the declarer, having drawn trumps, may be able to throw his losers. It is vital to attack the unbid suits immediately, in an attempt to establish tricks before declarer can dislodge your A♣. To this end, a spade looks best, since partner need hold only the queen or ace for it to be a winning lead. Recommended lead: 2♠.

c)   This elementary auction reveals that dummy is balanced and is unlikely to contain either a ruffing value or a long suit. The declarer may have to rely upon finesses and mis-defence to make extra tricks. You must find a safe lead. A trump is a possibility, but a diamond combines safety with a modest attempt to establish tricks. Lead J♦.

Notice that, from the same hand, there are three different leads, depending upon the auction. If you are not certain of the auction or you need it explained, ask to hear it again and cross-examine (politely) your opponents as to their understanding of their partner's bids. This you can and should do before making your opening lead.

Selecting Your Card
Having decided which suit you will lead, it is important to ensure that you pick the correct card, since this will inform your partner about your holding, your intentions, and whether you would like the suit returned to you. What follow are standard lead-agreements for bridge players the world over not only for opening leads, but for leads later in the hand also. Some people do play different methods and, if you are sitting down for a whole session with a new partner, it will be worth discussing your styles of play to check that they are similar.

Top-of-a-Sequence
This should be your favourite lead since it combines attack with safety. Against suit contracts, you will usually lead from just two honour cards in a row, whereas against no-trumps you require three cards involved. The lowest sequence is 1097. Lower sequences should merely be viewed as low cards.

These can be led against suit contracts:

KQxx   KQJx   QJ8x   KQx   J10xxx   AKxx

If you hold AK doubleton, most players agree to lead K, then A, to indicate that you hold only two cards in the suit.

Internal Sequence
This is a sequence inside a suit – with a higher, non-touching, card above the sequence. Against a suit contract, you would not lead an internal sequence from a suit headed by the ace – you would not lead that suit at all. Against NTs, where the length of the suit is its strength and it does not matter so much giving away a quick trick if your suit becomes established in the long run, leading from a suit headed by an ace is perfectly acceptable. Your partner may not be certain whether your lead is top-of-a-sequence or top-of-an-internal-sequence but, usually, his own hand and dummy will reveal the truth.

KJ109x   Q109xx   and, against NTs,   AJ1085

Leading from an Honour
A key understanding of basic card-play is that the lead of a low card indicates an interest in your partner trying to win the trick and returning the suit to you as soon as possible. This is because the lead of a low card indicates that you hold an honour card or cards at the head of the suit. The standard lead is "fourth highest"; when you hold only three cards, it should be the bottom one.

KJxx   Kxxx   Qxxxx   Q10xxx   Kxx   Qxx   Q10x   J9xx

Again, do not lead from a suit headed by an ace against suit contracts, but against NT contracts, it is just fine.

DON'T DO THIS ☞ Axx Axxx AJxxx or Axx Axxx

Just leave the suit alone and wait for declarer or partner to lead it to you. Against NT contracts, from each of these holdings, lead fourth highest as usual (or bottom from 3-to-an-honour).

Top-of-Rubbish
Given that a low intermediate card indicates interest in the suit, then, conversely, when you hold no honour cards in the suit you have decided to lead, you must lead a high card to indicate to your partner your lack of interest in the suit. Usually, this will be the second highest or, if that card seems low, play your highest card to make the message clear.

9752 10852 8432 987 98765

Notice that 10s, without a higher honour or the 9, are not honour cards and that sequences below 1097 are not regarded as important enough to indicate.

Most of the above leads are correct against NT contracts also but see page 136 for variations and additional leads.

Trumps
Your standard policy should always be to lead your lowest trump. This allows for partner holding a singleton or doubleton high card which might promote a trick later for you.
   The one exception to this might be when your holding in trumps is Ax or Axx and the auction suggests that leading trumps quickly is the winning defensive strategy. Then you would lead ace and a little one to get two rounds played as quickly as possible.

Leading Your Partner's Bid Suit
You had better have a pretty good reason for not leading a suit bid by partner! Because, unless you make a brilliant decision, he

will whine all night about how you didn't lead his suit.

Seriously though, if you choose not to lead partner's suit, it will be because you hold a singleton in another suit, or you are void in his suit or, possibly, you hold the ace in his suit and you are afraid to lead it or from it, in case the declarer holds the king and scores a cheap trick.

Once you have decided that you will lead partner's suit, follow all the above rules. You can lead a doubleton if your partner has bid the suit, and you should always lead the higher of two cards.

Don't be seduced by the old-fashioned biddies who tell you to lead the top card in your partner's suit whatever you hold. Except in rare circumstances this is very wrong. Remember the key communication element: the lead of a low card indicates interest in the suit; a high card lack of interest and the lead of an honour shows top-of-a-sequence. Occasionally when you are leading your partner's suit you will have to lead a doubleton honour card: it is up to partner to work out what is happening in his suit.

With this information you should have an idea of what style of lead you might want to make and then, having chosen it, know the correct card to lead to give your partner some information about your holding in the suit. Your partner will be watching your lead very carefully. As your standard increases, you and your partner will be able to use that lead, plus the view of dummy, combined with information from the auction, to determine what offers the best chance of defeating declarer and what his hand – and your partner's hand – might look like.

It is also important to have some basic signalling rules so that you can pass on important information to your partner about the line of play you feel you should take. We will examine these a little later on. There are many different styles but we will adopt the three most important and, unlike many players who make life much more difficult than it need be, we will use them for both suit contracts and no-trump contracts. Even if you are unable to interpret the information shown by these cards now, as you get used to the style of play and you have more time to study closely the cards the declarer and your partner are playing, you will be able to use this information to form a much clearer idea of the hidden hands. Once you can do that, you will be heading for the realms of skilful player.

Leading a Singleton
One of the most common leads against a suit contract is a singleton. As you have agreed not to lead a doubleton unless your partner has called the suit, your partner will know that it is a singleton and, if possible, he will win the trick and return the suit for a ruff.

When you hold two or three small trumps, which will not make a natural trump trick, leading your shortage is perfect. When you hold four trumps, however, you should not lead a shortage but instead attack your own side's longest suit, hoping to shorten the declarer's trump holding and put him out of control.

A singleton as an opening lead is dandy but, even if led later in the play of the hand, you may still get the chance to play a singleton and, subsequently score a ruff, but you have to be alert to that opportunity or it may just disappear . . .

Hand 34   Dealer North

N	E	S	W
1D	NB	1S	NB
2D	NB	4S	

♠ K6
♥ 103
♦ KQJ986
♣ QJ10

♠ 3   ♠ 10542
♥ KQ942   ♥ A765
♦ 5432   ♦ A
♣ 952   ♣ 7643

♠ AQJ987
♥ J8
♦ 107
♣ AK8

West leads K♥; what should East play, and why?

East should realise that West's lead is from a heart suit headed by king, queen and also that, unless the defence is dynamic, declarer will draw trumps and pitch his losers on dummy's long diamond suit. East holds a singleton A♦ but, if he plays it, can he get his partner back in to give him a ruff? Yes. East should overtake West's K♥ with his A♥, cash his A♦, and then return a heart to West's Q♥. If West doesn't realise that East's A♦ is a singleton, then East needs a new bridge partner, since it would be madness to set up dummy's long suit unless a ruff was imminent. West returns a diamond and the contract is scuppered.

Forcing Defence

One of the most common defences to a suit contract is where you lead passively and make declarer trump in his own hand. At the very least this makes him use up trumps which he would have scored at the end of the hand anyway and stops you from switching from suit to suit, helping the declarer. At best, it attacks the declarer at the very heart of his strength – his trump suit. When you hold four trumps, it is almost always wrong to lead a shortage since, if you can make the force bite, the declarer will be rendered helpless.

Hand 35   Dealer South

N	E	S	W
–	–	1H	NB
1S	NB	3H	NB
4H			

Look at North-South's trump holding. Surely West can make no more than one natural trump trick? Watch what happens . . .

West leads J♣ – his own longest suit – declarer plays low from dummy, so East allows it to hold the trick. West continues with 10♣ and that runs to South, who ruffs. South now holds 5 trumps to West's 4. Declarer crosses to dummy with Q♠ and leads 10♥, which runs around to West's king. West leads another club, East plays K♣ and declarer trumps in hand again.

Hand 35   *Dealer South*

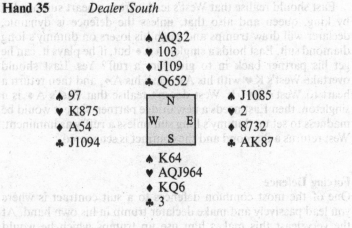

```
              ♠ AQ32
              ♥ 103
              ♦ J109
              ♣ Q652
  ♠ 97          N          ♠ J1085
  ♥ K875                    ♥ 2
  ♦ A54     W     E         ♦ 8732
  ♣ J1094        S          ♣ AK87
              ♠ K64
              ♥ AQJ964
              ♦ KQ6
              ♣ 3
```

Now, the relative trump holdings are: South 3; West 3. South cannot draw all West's trumps since he still has A♦ to lose, so he plays one more round of trumps to check the split and then stops. Next, he plays a diamond and West pounces with his A♦ and leads his last club. South trumps and now the relative trump lengths are: South 1; West 2! West has one more trump than South and must score that trick. South is defeated and there was nothing he could do about it.

> *Don't be afraid to let declarer trump in hand, but don't let him trump in dummy.*

In the rare situations when you recognize that dummy has more trumps than the declarer, you reverse that philosophy.

Trump Promotion

The trump suit is presumed to be the property of the declarer but that doesn't mean that you, as defenders, cannot muscle in on the action, even if you don't have four of them in one hand. Since you usually hold only four or five trumps between you, you may have to work hard to establish extra tricks, but that work will often pay dividends.

Hand 36   Dealer South

N	E	S	W
–	–	1S	NB
2C	NB	3S	NB
4S			

```
                    ♠ 642
                    ♥ J106
                    ♦ KQ
                    ♣ A7432
    ♠ AJ                          ♠ 107
    ♥ Q7432          N            ♥ AK5
    ♦ 1086        W     E         ♦ 97432
    ♣ J86            S            ♣ 1095
                    ♠ KQ9853
                    ♥ 98
                    ♦ AJ5
                    ♣ KQ
```

West leads 3♥ against South's game contract and East wins with
K♥, plays A♥ and leads a third heart which South trumps.
Declarer crosses to dummy with a low diamond to K♦ and then
leads 2♠ and runs it to his K♠. West wins with his A♠ and
wonders what to do next.

It seems unlikely that East now holds more than one or two
more points, since North-South are marked with at least 25pts
between them to be in game. Is there any hope for another
trick? If there is a club trick, East will make it later whatever
West does. But there is one positive try West can undertake. If
East were to hold 10♠, West might be able to promote his J♠
into the setting trick. So, certain that giving a ruff and discard
(see below) will not cost his side anything, he leads a fourth
round of hearts. Sure enough, East does ruff in with 10♠ and
declarer is, to use a not-very-technical bridge term, stuffed. If
he overruffs with Q♠, West's J♠ is the defence's fourth trick; if
he refuses to overruff, that's the fourth trick already. A classic
trump promotion.

"Ruff and Discard"? When you lead a suit in which both dummy and declarer is void, you allow the declarer to ruff in one hand and discard a loser from the other. To allow this to happen is usually very poor defence since it can allow unmakable contracts a chance to get home. However, if you are certain that the declarer will have no losers to throw away, and you and your partner still hold trumps which could be promotable, it is an acceptable and sometimes devastating line of defence. But, be careful.

Counting from the Auction

The auction should be in your mind throughout the play of the hand, and you should attempt to imagine what the declarer's hand looks like. This is easier than trying to picture your partner's hand since, as you are the defending side, he will almost certainly have done less bidding than the opposition. If you are paying attention, the right thing to do sometimes becomes blindingly obvious, but only if you've been paying attention . . .

Hand 37   Dealer South

N	E	S	W
–	–	1D	NB
1H	NB	1S	NB
4S			

```
                    ♠ A1064
                    ♥ AK53
                    ♦ QJ4
                    ♣ 74
        ♠ 73          N          ♠ J52
        ♥ 42      W       E      ♥ QJ1076
        ♦ 108632      S          ♦ –
        ♣ AK103                  ♣ J9862
                    ♠ KQ98
                    ♥ 98
                    ♦ AK975
                    ♣ Q5
```

West leads A♣ – the unbid suit – and surveys dummy while the declarer makes his plan. The auction – assuming that North-South are playing Acol, with a Weak NT (as most players in the UK will do) – reveals that South holds five diamonds and four spades. This means that, adding in North's 3-card diamond suit, East is void. By now, you can bet that South will have that cat-who's-had-all-the-cream look on his face, but that is about to change. At trick two, West leads a diamond and East ruffs. Realizing that West's initial lead must have been from ♣AK, East returns a club; West takes the trick with his K♣ and leads a second diamond for East to ruff. And that shows South that, at bridge, nothing is a sure thing until the tricks are in the bag.

Signals and Discards

There is as much information exchanged between partners in the defence as there is in the auction. This is done through following the standard lead agreements, signalling and discarding. You can choose to adopt with which of the following you play but, ideally, you'll go for everything which is mentioned below. Introduce each element to your system slowly and it will all make sense.

Generally, it is understood that a **signal** is information conveyed by a card played in the suit that has been led, whereas a **discard** occurs when you cannot follow suit and you throw away a card in another suit. Your choice of suit and card indicates with which other suit you want your partner to play. Both these techniques can, and should, be applied to both trump contracts and NT contracts.

Ace is for Attitude
An attitude signal is simply where you tell your partner what you think of his lead. You encourage or discourage him from leading further cards in the suit so that tricks are not given away by cashing top cards too early. To help our frazzled memories, I propose that we encourage and discourage like this in only one situation: when the ace is involved.

That is to say, when your partner leads an ace, if you like that lead and want him to lead his king (which he has promised) you will play the highest card you can afford.

On the other hand, if you do not want him to continue leading the suit, you play your lowest card in that suit. Hence, when encouraging and discouraging:

HIGH card encourages
LOW card discourages

You should also show attitude when your partner leads a suit and the second hand to play (either dummy or declarer) plays his ace. Again, if you liked your partner's lead, you should encourage; if you disliked, discourage.

When will you want to encourage and when will it be right to discourage? Thankfully, it is a simple matter. Taking the lead of an ace by your partner as an example, this is how you should think when defending a trump contract:

Partner has led the ace, promising the king. You would only want your partner to lead his king on the second round if you could win the third round, either because you hold the queen, or because you have a doubleton which would, if partner led two rounds, become a void allowing you to trump the third round.

At all other times, you would not want your partner to lead the king since this risks promoting a trick for the declarer.

Similarly, if dummy or declarer hops up with the ace, you should encourage only when you hold the king or queen, or you hold a doubleton in the suit which your partner might be able to utilize for ruffs.

For signalling against NT contracts, see page 175.

Enough talk, let's see some action. You are West against the declarer, South:

Hand 38   Dealer South

N	E	S	W
–	–	1S	NB
3S	NB	4S	

Your opponents have bid confidently to game. A reasonably attacking lead is called for and, thankfully, West holds an ace-king sequence in an unbid suit.

Hand 38   *Dealer South*

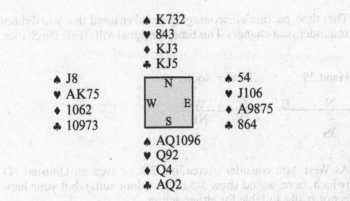

```
                      ♠ K732
                      ♥ 843
                      ♦ KJ3
                      ♣ KJ5
   ♠ J8              ┌─────────┐        ♠ 54
   ♥ AK75            │    N    │        ♥ J106
   ♦ 1062            │ W     E │        ♦ A9875
   ♣ 10973           │    S    │        ♣ 864
                     └─────────┘
                      ♠ AQ1096
                      ♥ Q92
                      ♦ Q4
                      ♣ AQ2
```

You lead A♥ rather than 10♣ since the lead of the ace allows you to retain control of the hand. When dummy comes down, your pulse quickens a little: it is a very flat hand, so declarer will not be able to ruff or establish a long suit – he may be in trouble. Careful defence is called for, to avoid giving the declarer cheap tricks. On the lead of A♥, East drops 6♥. Is that low or high? It all depends on the context. You look at your own hand and dummy and even the card the declarer played (if East has already grabbed the trick, at Rubber and Chicago, you can ask to look at it before a member of your side leads to the next trick). Declarer dropped 2♥, dummy has ♥43, you hold 5♥, so East's 6♥ was low, discouraging you from leading your K♥. You decide that the safest lead at trick two is a trump, so you lead 8♠.

You have just defeated the contract!

What did you do? You avoided giving the declarer a trick, and that is the only way he could have succeeded. If you had led K♥, observe what happens: declarer loses that trick, but his Q♥ is now a winner. He has only A♦ to lose and he has his ten tricks. By your not leading K♥, declarer faces two further heart losers and

A♦. When your partner wins A♦, he will switch straight back to hearts (he knows that you hold the king) and you will take two tricks there. In fact, the only way declarer could possibly make his Q♥ was if you had blindly led out both A♥ and K♥.

That is why it is so important to watch your partner's signals.

That time, partner's discouraging signal ensured that you did not squander your chances. This time, the signal will create the chance:

Hand 39   Dealer South

N	E	S	W
–	–	1S	NB
3S			

As West, you consider overcalling 2D, or even an Unusual NT (which, here, would show 5-5 in the minor suits), but your hand is not really suitable for either action.

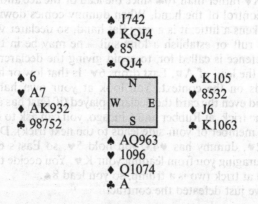

You lead A♦ and watch for partner's card. He plays J♦ which certainly seems high and therefore encouraging. He probably would not have encouraged if he had held Q♦, since he can see only two diamonds in dummy and would know that his queen could be ruffed, so it looks as though he holds a doubleton. You lead K♦; partner plays 6♦, so you lead a third diamond. Declarer ruffs with J♠ in dummy, but East overruffs with K♠ and returns a heart to your ace. You lead a fourth round of diamonds and dummy ruffs with 7♠, but East overruffs with 10♠ and the contract has been defeated.

That is first class defence. Declarer has four natural losers, so he looked on course for success. Your two ruffs on top of ♦AK and A♥ set the contract. But, wasn't it lucky that, having ruffed the diamond, your partner led a heart to your ace, rather than a club, which would have been fatal to the defence?

This hand illustrates how useful it is to be able to indicate in which suit(s) you hold high cards. The suggested method is **Suit-Preference**, sometimes also called "Mckenney". This method can be adopted for both signals and discards and, using it, West could have told East that his outside entry was in hearts rather than clubs. Then, it would not have been lucky that East-West set South's contract, it would have been a certainty based on pure skill.

Discards

When you cannot follow suit and you are deciding what card should be thrown away, always pick the suit in which you have least interest.

In other words, throw away what you do not want.

Suit-Preference Discards and Signals

Suit-preference is simple, powerful and easy to learn. As defenders, it will give you the confidence to communicate with one another using otherwise insignificant cards. It can be used both as a discarding style and as a signal. The principle is the same in both cases, although the execution is slightly different.

SP Discards

When you cannot follow suit, you throw a card from the suit in which you are least interested. However, the card you choose can perform a vital purpose. The first time that you discard is the most important; later discards are likely to be made under pressure and may contain no further information.

As you are throwing a card away from the suit in which you have least interest, it will probably make no difference to you whether you throw a low or a high card. However, whenever good bridge players have a choice of cards from which to play, their decision becomes significant.

For this reason, when you make your first discard, your partner knows this is the suit which you do not want him to lead. If he wishes to continue leading his own suit, that is his decision, but if he is considering a switch, your discard will act as a guide.

Discounting the trump suit, there will be at most three suits remaining. Since you will throw away a card from the suit you are least interested in, the SP discard will indicate which of the other two suits you would like led. This works just as well in no-trump contracts and should be adopted for all defensive play.

- To ask for the higher-ranking of the remaining two suits, you discard a HIGH card.
- To ask for the lower-ranking of the remaining two suits, you discard a LOW card.

Let's see an example:

Hand 40   Dealer South

N	E	S	W
–	–	1S	NB
3S	NB	4S	

West leads Q♥. Declarer plays low from dummy and wins in hand with K♥. He now leads K♠ and you decide to duck this trick because, as East is likely only to hold one trump, you will get a chance to see an informative discard on the second round of trumps. Declarer continues with a low trump and you hop up with your A♠ and watch for partner's card. East plays 9♥. This confirms what you pretty much know – he doesn't want you to lead a heart. But the size of East's card is the key element here.

By playing a high heart, he has asked for the higher-ranking of
the remaining two suits: in this case, a diamond rather than a
club. (If he had wanted a club, he would have played his lowest
heart.)

Hand 40   *Dealer South*

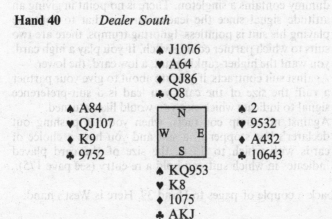

```
              ♠ J1076
              ♥ A64
              ♦ QJ86
              ♣ Q8
  ♠ A84          N          ♠ 2
  ♥ QJ107      W   E        ♥ 9532
  ♦ K9           S          ♦ A432
  ♣ 9752                    ♣ 10643
              ♠ KQ953
              ♥ K8
              ♦ 1075
              ♣ AKJ
```

Now, you switch to K♦. This holds the trick. You lead 9♦. East
wins this second diamond trick, realises that you have played a
doubleton because he asked you to lead the suit (you would have
played a low card from three or more cards to the king), and
returns the suit for you to ruff and set the contract.

Notice that East could have provided the same message by
throwing a low club, saying that he does not want a club led, but
instead the lower ranking out of hearts and diamonds – namely
diamonds. Using SP discards, you will almost always have two
ways to ask for what you want and that means you are very
likely to have the right card for the job.

To watch for these discards all through the hand would be too
tall an order, so the key moment to watch for is the first time
partner cannot follow suit and therefore makes a discard: that is
the one that will tell you where partner's strength lies.

SP Signals
There are only three key occasions when you make a suit-preference signal:

1.   Against suit contracts, when partner leads an ace and
      dummy contains a singleton. There is no point in giving an
      attitude signal since the leader can see that to continue
      playing his suit is pointless. Ignoring trumps, there are two
      suits to which partner could switch. If you play a high card,
      you want the higher-ranking suit; a low card, the lower.
2.   Against suit contracts, if you are about to give your partner
      a ruff, the size of the card you lead is a suit-preference
      signal to indicate which suit you would like returned.
3.   Against no-trump contracts, when you are pushing out
      declarer's last stopper in a suit and you have a choice of
      cards with which to do it, the size of the card played
      indicates in which suit you hold a re-entry (see page 175).

Flip back a couple of pages to Hand 39. Here is West's hand:

West
♠ 6
♥ A7
♦ AK932
♣ 98752

Remember that you, as West, led ♦AK and, seeing that partner
was almost certainly going to ruff, you led a third diamond. It
makes no difference to you which diamond you led since it was
going to be ruffed. But, for East, the card you chose was of vital
importance, since it would indicate which suit you wanted led
back to you once East had ruffed and taken the trick. On this
hand, you should lead 9♦ at trick three: a high card asking for the
higher of the remaining two suits to be returned. The trump suit –
spades – and diamonds themselves are discounted, leaving East to
choose the higher-ranking suit from hearts and clubs. He recog-
nizes the signal and knows that it is right to return a heart. That
allows you to regain the lead and provide the setting ruff for East.

Had you wanted a club to be returned, you should have led your
lowest diamond for East to ruff.

This all takes a great deal of concentration and focus by both players to make it work and, at first, you may find that it doesn't click. My advice would be to continue practising making the signals and discards and slowly you will find that you do have time to notice them. When that happens, your confidence will grow enormously and no contract will ever seem unbeatable again.

Forming a Picture of the Hand
The greatest step any bridge player takes is to attempt to form a picture of all four hands, using information from the auction and the early play to try to place missing cards and decide on the winning course of action. One way that you, as defenders, can improve your skills in this area – when you are not involved in trying to win the trick – is by following suit, playing count signals.

Count Signals
Thus, when you are neither leading nor involved in trying to win the trick, you should try to give partner a count on your holding in that suit. These signals are equally important when defending both suit contracts and NT contracts:

- Playing a high card, followed by a low card, shows an even number of cards held in the suit.
- Playing a low card, followed by a high card, shows an odd number of cards in the suit.

However, since you often only get one chance to indicate your holding in a suit, partner will be watching your first card very closely and will assume that a high card means an even number of cards; a low card an odd number of cards.

Why would you need to show count? Well, there are many times when the fact that partner knows how many cards you hold in the suit is pretty irrelevant but it is well to get into good habits, because the more you know about your partner's hand, the more you can deduce about the declarer's hand until, sometimes, you can almost see it in your mind's eye. The most important time to be aware of the count situation is when dummy contains a good suit with no side entries. At this stage, it will be vital to assess your course of action in line with the information you have on the layout of the suit.

Hand 41   Dealer North

N	E	S	W
NB	NB	2NT	NB
3NT			

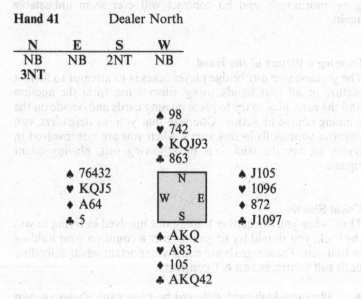

```
                          ♠ 98
                          ♥ 742
                          ♦ KQJ93
                          ♣ 863
         ♠ 76432                        ♠ J105
         ♥ KQJ5          N              ♥ 1096
         ♦ A64        W     E           ♦ 872
         ♣ 5             S              ♣ J1097
                          ♠ AKQ
                          ♥ A83
                          ♦ 105
                          ♣ AKQ42
```

West leads K♥ and declarer can count three spade, a heart and three club tricks. If the clubs split well or he can make two diamond tricks, he will be home.

From East's point of view, he has two key responsibilities: firstly, he must keep hold of his four clubs – his only decent suit. Secondly, dummy's diamonds look very strong but, if declarer does not hold A♦, it may be possible to seal the declarer out of dummy. It will be essential for East to indicate how many cards in the diamond suit he holds so that, by looking at his own hand and dummy, West can then work out how many diamonds declarer holds in his hand. This information will allow West to judge when to play his A♦ (if he has it) and when to hold up. Best defence will ensure that South makes only the diamond tricks to which he is entitled and not any more.

South ducks the first trick, East contributing 6♥ (low card showing an odd number) and West continues with Q♥. Declarer wins this with A♥ and lays down ♣AK. West discards a spade on the second club (the suit in which he is least interested). Declarer switches his attention to diamonds, leading 10♦ from hand. West plays 4♦, dummy 3♦, and East 2♦. Now, declarer leads 5♦ from hand. What should West do?

If he ducks this trick, declarer will make a second diamond trick and make his contract. Instead, West should remember that East played 2♦ on the first round of the suit – a low card indicating an odd number of cards held. If he only holds one diamond, then South has four and West is powerless. But, if East holds three diamonds, then South holds only two and West must rise with A♦ now. He does so, cashes two heart winners, and then gets off lead with a spade. Declarer has only eight tricks and must concede a club to East. One down.

Without the count signals, West would have been guessing when to play his A♦ and when to duck. And guessing is just no good anymore.

These principles apply equally in suit contracts and in no-trump contracts.

Background Thoughts in Defence
As I hope you have seen, your defence will vary considerably depending upon the auction, what you see in dummy and the declarer's play. There are, however, some basic rules which apply much – if not all – of the time. They are worth having in the back of your mind:

1.   Second hand to play usually plays low; third hand to play usually plays high, trying to win the trick or to push out high cards.

If you leap in with high cards when you are second to play, it gives declarer a chance to play low from his other hand. It is usually best to leave your partner – who will be in fourth seat – to decide whether to win or duck. This also avoids the possibility that you will crash your high card under or on top of your partner's high card. Of course, if you have a specific reason for wanting to gain the lead, then you may try to win the trick, but try to check whether your partner may be short and have to play a high card himself.

2.   Lead up to weakness on your right.

This is so that the final hand to play (the one on your right) is unlikely to be able to beat whatever your partner plays. This ensures that the declarer has to commit himself before your partner has to decide what to do.

This is easy for the player with the dummy on his right – he can see the hand – but, for the player with declarer on his right, he must work out from the auction and from signals given by his partner, which suit will be safest.

3.   Never lead dummy's long suit.

The word never is a bit silly because there are always exceptions – that's why bridge is such a great game. However, since it will be right only about once a year to lead dummy's long suit, never is a pretty good description. Why not lead dummy's long suit? Because it is just what the declarer wants you to do to get his suit established – and doing what the declarer wants us to do is not on our agenda.

Above all, most defences are about not giving away tricks, so meditate on that thought the next time you wonder what to play.

When defending suit contracts, the vast majority of the time you are *not* trying to make tricks. You are attempting to use your high cards to take your opponents' high cards and prevent declarer from making tricks.

4

KEY STRATEGY FOR NO-TRUMP PLAY

No-trump play strikes terror into the hearts of the nervous but, in many ways, it can be more relaxing than playing with a trump suit. In a suit contract, there are usually myriad possibilities, second chances, and last ditch efforts. In no-trumps, whether you are declarer or defender, you usually need to find the right line immediately and then stick to it doggedly.

No-trump play is about tricks: how many you and the dummy contains, how many more you require, from where you will find them, and what state your defences are in, particularly in the case of the suit that your opponents have attacked from the off. It is a race between defenders and declarer to establish their side's long suit, and it is a race I am determined that you will – in this chapter at least – win! When we come to defending, I'll want you to win that race, but that's the beauty of the challenge – it's so close and so much difference can be made by just a few seemingly insignificant things.

Foresight is a vital commodity in bridge but no more so than when playing and defending no-trump contracts. Anticipating who might win what trick and what he might do subsequently is essential. Within this section, your powers of foresight will be stimulated, the concept of danger hands will be introduced, and the means to win the race will be revealed. Hopefully, by the end of the following section, you will enjoy the prospect of playing in no-trumps – at least until you read the next section after that – on defending no-trumps . . .

Basic Strategy

When the lead is made against your no-trump contract, trick counting becomes a mantra for the declarer, just as it should be for the defenders.

From the moment dummy hits baize you, as declarer, should first count how many top tricks (tricks you could cash without losing the lead) you hold between your hand and dummy. Second, subtract that total from the number of tricks that you require to make your contract. Finally, decide from which suit (or suits) you are going to try to establish those extra tricks.

At this stage, depending upon your skills, you should consider what your opponent's lead is indicating, whether one opponent provides a greater threat than the other, and whether your first plan is a fast enough one to succeed against the best efforts of your opponents. During the forthcoming examples, we will look at each of these scenarios.

For the defence, it will usually be from the suit they have led that the power to break the contract will be derived. Generally, the defence should attack with their longest suit and continue attacking. Rarely, it will be right to find a killing switch to another suit but, since the one advantage the defenders have against NT contracts is that they get to lead their long suit first, switching from suit to suit tends to be a sure sign of defender desperation.

5

NO-TRUMP CONTRACTS – FOCUS ON DECLARER PLAY

The Hold-Up

Most social bridge players know of the importance, in no-trump contracts, of retaining control in each suit, and not cashing winning cards until there are sufficient to fulfil the contract. But, for what reason do you refuse to play your winner until a later (or the last) moment?

This is a classic hold-up play, and you are the declarer in the South seat.

Hand 42   Dealer South

N	E	S	W
–	–	1NT	NB
3NT			

West leads K♠ and you, as South, make your basic plan. You have one spade trick, two heart tricks, three diamond tricks and, as yet, no club tricks. That is six top tricks, leaving three more to be found. Clearly, once A♣ is dislodged, that suit will provide at least three more. So, your basic plan is to push out A♣ as soon as possible and then cash the winners.

Hand 42   *Dealer South*

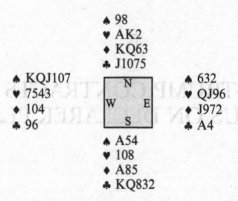

```
              ♠ 98
              ♥ AK2
              ♦ KQ63
              ♣ J1075
♠ KQJ107            N            ♠ 632
♥ 7543                           ♥ QJ96
♦ 104       W         E          ♦ J972
♣ 96                S            ♣ A4
              ♠ A54
              ♥ 108
              ♦ A85
              ♣ KQ832
```

What might stop that plan? West has led top-of-a-sequence in spades – your weakest suit. Once A♠ is gone, there will be nothing to stop East-West from running through their spade tricks. To attempt to disrupt this simple defence, you must try a hold-up play. You duck the first round of spades, allowing West to win. When West continues with Q♠, again you refuse the trick. Finally, on the third round, you have no choice but to win. However, look at the effect of the hold-up: East holds no more spades. So, when East wins A♣, he cannot return a spade to West and must break open a new suit. Since you have control of all the other suits, you can win, and make the rest of the tricks.

Of course, if West had held A♣, the hold-up would have been in vain, and the contract in tatters. But that would be its fate no matter what you did. 3NT would be unmakable.

So, in simple terms, the purpose of the hold-up play is to exhaust one opponent of his supply of the suit, cutting communications between the opponents' hands.

Rule of 7
I hate rules. They have nothing whatsoever to do with trying to play good bridge. It is essential to understand why you do things

at the table: a crib-sheet is actually counter-productive. Here, however, when there are many other things on your mind, is a simple aide-memoire – until you feel confident enough to work out exactly why you are doing it.

To fulfil the Rule of 7:

Total the number of cards between you and dummy in the suit about which you are worried, subtract that total from seven, and the answer is the number of times you should hold-up (not play) your single stopper.

For example, in hand 42, declarer held three spades, and dummy two spades. Take that total of five away from seven, and you are left with two. Therefore, declarer should hold-up two times. Accordingly, South did duck twice, East was exhausted of spades, and declarer prevailed.

The purpose of the rule is to help you to judge how many times it is necessary to hold-up to exhaust an opponent if their suit is splitting poorly. If it is splitting evenly, you are unlikely to be able to exhaust one opponent and, since neither opponent holds any great length, it is probably unnecessary anyway.

Analyse the Lead
If your opponent has not led the suit in which you are weakest, it will usually be right not to duck the first trick, since that will provide a chance for your opponent to switch to a suit you fear more. Indeed, even if you hold only one stopper in the suit led, there will be times when, having analysed the lead, you realise that holding up is quite unnecessary.

Hand 43   **Dealer South**

N	E	S	W
–	–	1NT	NB
3NT			

Hand 43   *Dealer South*

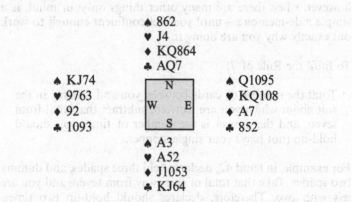

♠ 862
♥ J4
♦ KQ864
♣ AQ7

♠ KJ74   ♠ Q1095
♥ 9763   ♥ KQ108
♦ 92   ♦ A7
♣ 1093   ♣ 852

♠ A3
♥ A52
♦ J1053
♣ KJ64

West led 4♠ and East played his Q♠. Declarer felt that, since he held only one stopper in the suit, he had better hold-up. However East, holding what he felt would be the key card on the hand – A♦ (which is preventing South from enjoying dummy's long diamond suit) – decided that he could attack his own long suit quite safely and be certain of defeating declarer. So, at trick two, East switched to K♥ and now South was in the same situation all over again – but having lost a trick already. He held up his ace for a couple of rounds in hearts and then, craftily, East switched back to spades. Now, when South won his A♠ and pushed out East's A♦, East could continue leading spades and the contract failed by two tricks.

What South had omitted to do before deciding how to play was to analyse the lead. East-West were, like most pairs, playing fourth highest leads (see page 143) and West's 4♠ was the lowest card he could hold (since 2♠ was in dummy and 3♠ in declarer's hand). Therefore, West could hold no more than four spades (he can't have a fifth highest card in his hand). Knowing that the spade suit was splitting 4–4 and fearing that the defence might switch to hearts, South should take his A♠ immediately. He pushes out East's A♦ and East-West can cash three more spade tricks. But that is all. When they switch to hearts, South wins, enjoys his clubs and diamonds and makes his contract.

Avoidance

On hand 42, declarer held up his single spade stopper until East was exhausted of spades and then he had to hope that it would be East who won A♣ and could not lead any further spades. Often, you can do more than simply hope. By skilful play, you can engineer it that only one opponent – the opponent who is exhausted of the danger suit, or who cannot profitably attack your weaknesses – can win a trick, whilst the dangerous opponent (or "danger hand" as it is often known) cannot gain the lead at all. Take a look at these examples:

Hand 44   **Dealer South**

N	E	S	W
–	–	1NT	NB
3NT			

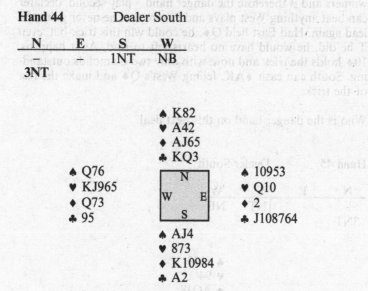

```
              ♠ K82
              ♥ A42
              ♦ AJ65
              ♣ KQ3
  ♠ Q76       ┌─────┐      ♠ 10953
  ♥ KJ965     │  N  │      ♥ Q10
  ♦ Q73       │W   E│      ♦ 2
  ♣ 95        │  S  │      ♣ J108764
              └─────┘
              ♠ AJ4
              ♥ 873
              ♦ K10984
              ♣ A2
```

West leads 6♥ and South makes his plan. He has two spade, a heart, two diamond and three club tricks. Eight tricks. He must find one more. The diamond suit looks promising. If Q♦ drops, the rest of the suit will be winners. Overtricks look likely here. Declarer applies the Rule of 7 to the heart suit (six hearts between his two hands, taken away from seven, leaves one) and holds up his A♥ for one round. When East continues leading hearts, South wins in dummy, knowing that either the suit is splitting evenly (4–3) or East has no hearts left. When he comes to play the diamond suit, this should be in his mind.

With nine cards headed by the ace-king, one usually cashes the top honours and hopes for the queen to fall (see page 43). If declarer took that line here, West would be left with Q♦ and the diamond suit would be dead. Even the spade finesse fails, and the contract follows soon afterwards.

Instead, at trick three, declarer leads 10♦ from hand and, when West correctly plays low, declarer should also play low from dummy. By making West – who holds the remaining heart winners and is therefore the danger hand – play second, declarer can beat anything West plays and ensure that he never gains the lead again. Had East held Q♦, he could win this trick but, even if he did, he would have no hearts left to lead. As it happens, 10♦ holds the trick and now, with only two diamonds outstanding, South can cash ♦AK, felling West's Q♦ and make the rest of the tricks.

Who is the danger hand on this next deal?

Hand 45   Dealer South

N	E	S	W
–	–	1NT	NB
3NT			

```
                    ♠ J109
                    ♥ 94
                    ♦ AQJ8
                    ♣ AK105
      ♠ K32          ┌─────┐        ♠ 876
      ♥ AJ863        │  N  │        ♥ 1075
      ♦ 964          │W   E│        ♦ K73
      ♣ 84           │  S  │        ♣ 9632
                     └─────┘
                    ♠ AQ54
                    ♥ KQ2
                    ♦ 1052
                    ♣ QJ7
```

West leads 6♥ and declarer assesses his position. He holds a spade trick, very soon at least one heart trick, a diamond and four club tricks. That is seven tricks, leaving two more to be found. Both spades and diamonds can provide those extra tricks once the missing king has been successfully finessed or lost. Before deciding on which suit to try, declarer plays out the first trick. East contributes 10♥ and declarer wins with Q♥. South now knows one key fact and, with it, he will base his entire strategy: West holds A♥. He knows this because, if East had held A♥ he would have played it at trick one. This is certain because (as described on page 80) when partner leads a low card he is asking his partner to try to win the trick and return the suit. South must now use that information to decide if one opponent is more dangerous than the other. What do you think?

Your gut reaction is probably to assume that West is the danger hand since he holds the length in hearts. However, South still holds ♥K2, so if West gets on lead and plays a heart, South's K♥ must take another trick. What would happen if East gained the lead and led a heart **through** South's ♥K2? Now, it would be curtains for South's K♥ and for his contract. West would beat whatever card he played and continue playing hearts until he had defeated the contract. So, on this hand, the opponent who can lead back to his partner's long suit is the more dangerous and he must not be allowed on lead.

If possible, make the danger hand play second to any key tricks – that way, whatever card he plays, you or dummy still have the chance to beat it and prevent that hand from winning the trick.

Here, to take a diamond finesse through West into East's hand would be far too dangerous, allowing East to play last. Instead, South must play on spades, making East play second and ensuring that only West can win a trick.

At trick two, declarer crosses to dummy by playing a club and then leads J♠. When East plays small, declarer can play low also, knowing that East cannot win the trick. Had the finesse been successful, South could have repeated it, but in fact West wins with K♠. If West leads another heart, he gives South another trick there; if he switches to, say, a diamond, declarer hops up with A♦, carefully cashes his spades and clubs and claims his contract.

Hand 46   Dealer South

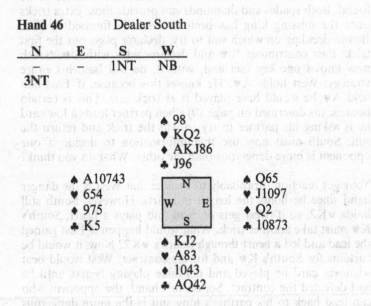

N	E	S	W
–	–	1NT	NB
3NT			

Another 3NT contract, another problem. West leads 4♠; South makes his plan. He has one spade trick (coming in a moment), three hearts, two diamonds and a club. That is seven tricks, leaving two more to be found. The diamond suit should provide the extra tricks, so all should be well.

The lead runs around to East's Q♠ and South wins with K♠. Again, the first trick reveals that East does not hold A♠ – or he would have played it – and so West still holds that card. As in the previous example, it is East who is the danger hand, since it is he who can lead through South's remaining ♠J2 and that will be the end of him. East must be kept off lead. This is awkward since any finesse in diamonds has to be taken into the East hand. With eight cards missing the queen, it is traditional to finesse, since it offers the better chance of not losing to the queen (see page 43). Here, however, if West holds Q♦ South can afford to lose the lead to him once (South's ♠J2 is still a stopper with West on lead) but he cannot afford to lose the lead to East.

At trick two then, South plays a diamond from hand and plays the ace and king, hoping that the queen falls. It does, and his remaining diamonds are all winners. If Q♦ had not fallen, South would have had to play a third round and hope that West held the queen. If East had started with ♦Qxx, South would have been helpless. However, the one thing declarer must not do is to finesse into the danger hand. If he does this, then 50% of the time the danger hand will win, return the suit about which declarer is concerned and the contract will fail. To re-iterate then:

Avoid taking a finesse into the danger hand.

If you find the concept of a danger hand difficult, lay out these example hands and play them through. Once you grasp it, you will find that it is a simple procedure to ascertain who presents the danger and then attempt to keep that hand off lead. It is a vital technique which occurs both in suit and no-trump contracts.

As simple guidelines, consider these:

If you hold up your stopper (following the Rule of 7) then, it will almost always be the leader, with the long suit, who will be the danger hand and his partner who will be the safe hand.

If you win the first round in the suit because you hold two honours, it will usually be the partner of the leader who is dangerous as he can lead the suit back **through** your remaining holding.

To add one more layer to the mysteries of avoidance, here is a technique that I have termed a **Stranding Play**. Instead of keeping a dangerous opponent off lead, you strand the safe opponent on lead. As before, the hand you wish to manipulate must be made to play second to the trick, allowing you or your dummy, to win or duck as you choose.

Hand 47   Dealer South

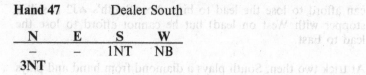

N	E	S	W
–	–	1NT	NB
3NT			

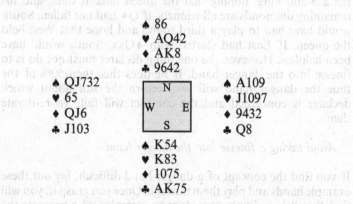

```
                 ♠ 86
                 ♥ AQ42
                 ♦ AK8
                 ♣ 9642
 ♠ QJ732      N        ♠ A109
 ♥ 65                  ♥ J1097
 ♦ QJ6    W     E      ♦ 9432
 ♣ J103        S       ♣ Q8
                 ♠ K54
                 ♥ K83
                 ♦ 1075
                 ♣ AK75
```

West leads 3♠. South has a spade (imminently), three heart, two diamond and two club tricks. Eight tricks is one short, but hearts might split 3–3 or the club suit might produce a third trick.

East plays A♠ and returns 10♠ (see page 154). Applying the Rule of 7, South ducks a second time (he had no choice but to duck on the first round) and wins the third round when East leads 9♠. It now appears that West holds two more spade winners and that East is void. East is the safe hand; West is dangerous. Since there is no finesse available in clubs, a stranding play is declarer's only hope. Since he wishes to strand East on play, he must ensure that East plays second to any key tricks.

Declarer crosses to dummy with A♦ and leads a low club. East plays 8♣, and South wins with A♣. South crosses back to dummy with a top heart and leads another low club, East producing Q♣. So, South . . . ducks – leaving East stranded on lead with his Q♣. When South regains the lead, he can cash the K♣ and the fourth round is established as his ninth trick.

What if East did not play Q♣ on the second round of clubs? South would have to win, test to see if hearts are 3–3 and, if they are not, he must then play a third round of clubs hoping that East has the final club. If all of this fails, the contract could not be made.

Incidentally, if East craftily plays Q♣ on the first round of the suit, South just ducks then. As long as Q♣ appears, South can arrange for it to win the trick, stranding East on lead – with no more spades in his hand.

Timing
No-trump play is all about timing. To judge in which order to play tricks is absolutely crucial and, in addition to the avoidance strategies shown earlier, requires foresight and concentration.

Hand 48   Dealer South

N	E	S	W
		1D	NB
3D	NB	3NT	

```
              ♠ Q103
              ♥ 54
              ♦ A1072
              ♣ A976
   ♠ A87         N         ♠ 9652
   ♥ QJ1096              ♥ 873
   ♦ 54      W     E      ♦ K86
   ♣ Q103       S         ♣ J82
              ♠ KJ4
              ♥ AK2
              ♦ QJ93
              ♣ K54
```

West leads Q♥ and declarer settles into trick-counting mode. He has two heart winners, a diamond and two clubs, leaving him with four further tricks to find. The spade suit will produce two extra tricks once A♠ is dislodged, the diamond suit two or three tricks depending on the fate of the finesse. However, to achieve this, declarer may have to lose the lead twice. Although he holds two heart stoppers, one will be dislodged immediately, and the second removed the moment he loses his first trick. Does it make any difference whether South attacks spades or diamonds first?

The two suits are different. The A♠ could be in either defender's hand whereas, if West holds K♦, he can never win the trick with it, since a diamond will always be finessed through him. Only East could win the trick with K♦. Thinking like this should lead declarer to realise that the diamond finesse is better taken later, once East has run out of hearts, whereas the A♠ needs to be dislodged quickly, in case West holds that card. So, declarer plays as follows.

He ducks the first heart lead – trying to exhaust East of his supply of the suit – and then wins the continuation. He now plays a spade which West probably ducks. Another spade is played and West wins and leads a third round of hearts. South uses his final stopper to win this trick and then leads Q♦ from hand, running it when West plays low. East wins with K♦ but, with no hearts left to lead, he must immediately concede the lead back to South who now has sufficient tricks for his contract.

Notice that if East had won K♦ while he still had hearts, the suit would have been cleared and, when West won A♠, he could cash enough tricks to defeat the contract.

After showing a hand like this, I am often asked how I could know where the outstanding high cards were located. I don't know. I assume that East holds K♦ because, if West holds it, the finesse will be successful and the contract cannot fail. It is possible however that West has led a short heart suit and it is East who holds the length. If that is the case, then this line fails. It's possible, but it is unlikely.

Anticipating the worst is often the way to safeguard your interests. I tend to think at bridge that when you see dummy, if everything looks promising, you should be pessimistic – looking for things that might go wrong and guarding against that happening; if everything looks grim, be optimistic, ask yourself what good things need to happen in order for you to succeed, and then play for those good things to happen.

On this next deal, declarer must be on the look-out from the start:

Hand 49   Dealer South

N	E	S	W
–	–	1D	NB
2C	NB	**3NT**	

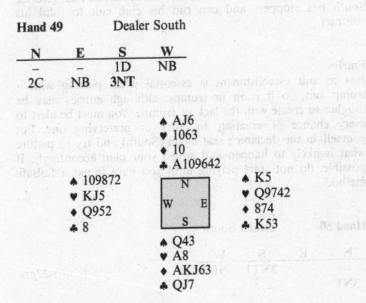

West leads 10♠ and declarer counts his tricks: a spade, a heart, two diamonds and a club. Five tricks; four more required. The club suit will provide those tricks and, with two stoppers in spades, it seems safe to play low from dummy. However, if South does play low, East will win with K♠ and, realizing that K♣ is a definite entry to his hand, he will switch smartly to a low heart, leading up to weakness on his right and trying to establish his own long suit. Now, declarer's A♥ stopper is dislodged before he has the club suit running for him. If South assumes the worst – that East holds K♠ and K♣ – he can play accordingly and still prevail.

At trick one, declarer realises that, if he rises with A♠ he still holds a stopper. He also prevents a possible heart switch about which he is far more concerned, since he only holds one stopper in that suit. He returns to hand with A♦ and then leads Q♣ running it when West plays small. East may duck to give the impression the finesse is working and hoping that South runs out of clubs in his hand, but South repeats the finesse with J♣ and this does lose to K♣. However, whichever suit East returns, South has stoppers and can run his club suit to fulfil his contract.

Entries

Just as suit establishment is essential when playing with a trump suit, so it is in no-trumps, although entries may be tougher to create with the lack of trumps. You must be alert to every chance of creating an entry or preserving one. Put yourself in the declarer's seat again (South) and try to picture what is likely to happen and adjust your plan accordingly. If possible, do not start playing until you have found a failsafe method.

Hand 50   Dealer South

N	E	S	W	
–	–	2NT†	NB	
3NT				† *20½-22pts*

♠ K6
♥ 873
♦ J10974
♣ Q73

♠ QJ109   ♠ 872
♥ Q954   ♥ J102
♦ K62   ♦ 83
♣ 85   ♣ K10942

♠ A543
♥ AK6
♦ AQ5
♣ AJ6

West leads Q♠ and you see that your six top tricks will need to be swollen by establishing the diamond suit. It seems obvious to win K♠ in dummy and take the diamond finesse, but West will duck. If you play another diamond to Q♦, West can win and you are stuck with the bare A♦ in hand and no means to return to dummy. You have blocked the suit. The simple solution is to preserve K♠ entry to dummy and abandon thoughts of finesses. You should win trick one in hand with A♠, lay down A♦, then Q♦ and, if that is ducked, 5♦ also. When West wins K♦, you as South have all the other suits covered and can cross back to dummy's K♠ and cash his winning diamonds.

On this next deal, declarer actually has to create an entry. In the driver's seat again, see if you can find the key play at trick one:

Hand 51   Dealer South

N	E	S	W
–	–	1H	NB
2D	NB	2NT	NB
3NT			

```
                        ♠ QJ6
                        ♥ 74
                        ♦ AK9854
                        ♣ 83
                       ┌─────────┐
                       │    N    │
          7♠ led       │ W     E │
                       │    S    │
                       └─────────┘
                        ♠ A54
                        ♥ AJ103
                        ♦ QJ
                        ♣ QJ107
```

When West leads 7♠, you can see that dummy's diamond suit is your main source of tricks and vital to the success of your contract. If the diamond suit does not split 3–2 however, you may be sealed off from those tricks. Can you ensure that there is an entry to dummy in another suit?

If you play Q♠ from dummy at trick one and East plays low, you are in dummy now. You can play a low diamond to Q♦ in hand and then plan to overtake J♦ with K♦. If the suit splits 4–1 (which it does here) you will have to lose a diamond trick and you will not be able to get back to the table.

The solution is to play a low spade from dummy at trick one and win with A♠ whatever East plays. Now, you cash ♦QJ, playing low both times from dummy. Now, play another spade. Whether East or West holds K♠, they will have to play it to stop you from reaching dummy immediately and, whatever they lead next, you will soon gain control and can then play your last spade over to dummy and enjoy the rest of your diamonds. Here's the full deal.

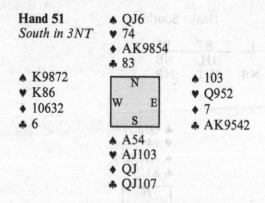

Hand 51
South in 3NT

♠ QJ6
♥ 74
♦ AK9854
♣ 83

♠ K9872
♥ K86
♦ 10632
♣ 6

♠ 103
♥ Q952
♦ 7
♣ AK9542

♠ A54
♥ AJ103
♦ QJ
♣ QJ107

Sometimes means of access is such a problem that there are no outside entries to create or preserve, so declarer will have to go one step further to ensure a successful suit establishment. Ducking often provides the means:

Hand 52   Dealer South

N	E	S	W	
–	–	1NT†	NB	† *Strong NT; 16–18pts*
2NT	NB	3NT		

Hand 52   *Dealer South*

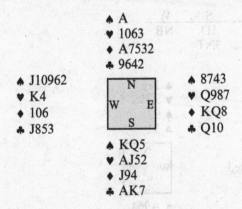

♠ A
♥ 1063
♦ A7532
♣ 9642

♠ J10962
♥ K4
♦ 106
♣ J853

♠ 8743
♥ Q987
♦ KQ8
♣ Q10

♠ KQ5
♥ AJ52
♦ J94
♣ AK7

When West leads J♠, declarer can count seven top tricks. The heart suit is most unlikely to produce two extra tricks, so the diamond suit must be established. However, with A♠ dislodged at trick one, the only entry to dummy is A♦ – and so that card must be preserved at all costs.

Declarer wins trick one with A♠ and leads a low diamond from dummy, won by East's Q♦, who is eager to return his partner's original lead. He returns a spade and South wins and plays another diamond from hand, again ducking in dummy. East probably wins this also. East may continue spades or try an aggressive heart switch but neither will work. South can win, play his last diamond to dummy's ace and then cash the extra two diamond tricks for his contract. If declarer touches dummy's A♦ before the third round, he is doomed.

However good the player, the basic planning should be the same. This next hand cropped up in a club teams event and both declarers thought themselves frightfully superior until, that is, they both failed in an easy contract. Put yourself in South's seat and see if you can do better – and don't forget to count your tricks.

Hand 53   Dealer South

N	E	S	W
–	–	1D	NB
1H	NB	3NT	

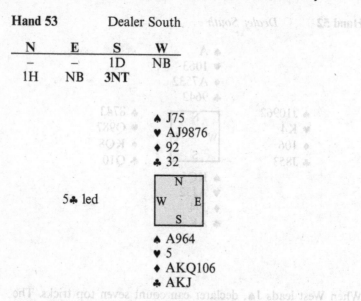

```
                    ♠ J75
                    ♥ AJ9876
                    ♦ 92
                    ♣ 32
                        N
   5♣ led           W       E
                        S
                    ♠ A964
                    ♥ 5
                    ♦ AKQ106
                    ♣ AKJ
```

1D seems a bit timid on South's lovely hand, but what is the
alternative? 1D probably is best and, when North drags up a bid,
at least the 3NT ensures game is not missed. West leads 5♣,
which is helpful to your cause but you still only have eight tricks.
From where will the ninth come?

Let's see what happened in the match. Both declarers won trick
one with J♣ and then laid down ♦AK. When West showed out
on the second round, South had to hope for a 3–3 spade break.
When that didn't materialize, the contract was down.

Let's return to basics: South has one spade, one heart, three
diamond and three club tricks – one short of the desired total.
The diamond suit must produce an extra trick, since between
dummy and his own hand, declarer holds five of the top six
cards. However, in case there are poor splits, declarer must make
use of dummy's 9♦ and not squander it under a top honour. At
trick two, South correctly leads a low diamond from hand to
dummy's 9♦ and East wins with J♦. Now, South's 10♦ has
become a certain trick and his contract is safe.

Here's the full deal:

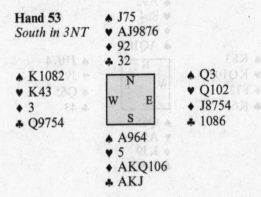

Hand 53
South in 3NT

♠ J75
♥ AJ9876
♦ 92
♣ 32

♠ K1082
♥ K43
♦ 3
♣ Q9754

♠ Q3
♥ Q102
♦ J8754
♣ 1086

♠ A964
♥ 5
♦ AKQ106
♣ AKJ

Often a contract comes down to locating a key card. Your opponents' bidding – or lack of it – opening lead or defensive strategy may point the way. As your confidence in the basic plays increases, you will have more time to look for the little details and create some magical plays of your own. Finding an opponent's card by using the subtlest of clues is immensely satisfying – take this example of negative inference . . .

Hand 54   Dealer West

N	E	S	W	
–	–	–	NB	† *with two tens, North is too*
1C†	NB	2NT‡	NB	*strong to open a Weak 1NT*
3NT				‡ *10–12pts, balanced*

West leads K♥ and declarer considers his situation. He has five top tricks and therefore needs four more. The club suit will produce two or three extra tricks and the diamond suit will give him one more if he can find out who holds Q♦ and finesse against that hand.

Hand 54   *Dealer West*

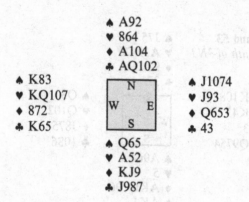

♠ A92
♥ 864
♦ A104
♣ AQ102

♠ K83
♥ KQ107
♦ 872
♣ K65

♠ J1074
♥ J93
♦ Q653
♣ 43

♠ Q65
♥ A52
♦ KJ9
♣ J987

South ducks one round of hearts (Rule of 7 again), East jettisoning his J♥ (see page 150). West leads Q♥ and South wins and leads 9♣. When West plays small, declarer plays low from dummy and the nine holds the trick. Now, South plays J♣ and again, when West plays small, dummy plays small also. Declarer can now cash his A♣, felling West's K♣ and play his fourth club. He still needs one extra trick and there are two possible ways of making it. He can hope that East holds K♠ and lead a low spade from dummy towards his Q♠, or he can guess who holds Q♦ and finesse against them. Since two-way finesses (finesses which can be taken through either opponent) should be left to the last possible moment in order to glean as much information as possible about the likely distribution, South leads a low spade from dummy first, playing Q♠ from hand and losing to West's K♠, West cashes his two heart winners and exits with another spade. South is still clinging on; he just has to find out who holds Q♦.

The answer lies in the auction. West dealt and passed. So what? Well, West has shown up with ♥KQ, K♠ and K♣, making eleven high-card points. He cannot also hold Q♦ or he would have opened the bidding. Therefore, East must hold that card. Declarer leads a low diamond from dummy, playing J♦ when East plays low. This holds the trick and his nine tricks are made.

Some readers will consider that counting out the opponents' points like that, remembering the auction, and drawing the winning conclusion, all seem a bit far-fetched but, I guarantee you, as you take more of the basic plays for granted, there will be space in your brain to work out tough stuff like that. And, boy, does it feel good.

Key Suit Holdings

If, like many bridge players, you find that seeing cards printed on the page is far less clear than having them in front of you on the table, then take the time to lay out the cards as shown below, particularly if any explanation does not seem logical. Then, following the guidance given, play the suits out and watch the effect for yourself. It really will make your bridge life – and that of your partners – a whole lot happier if you are relaxed and confident about these situations.

The first trick in no-trumps is often crucial, in terms of hold-up plays, entry preservation, even the creation of stoppers. There are some particularly important suit holdings upon which it is worth reflecting. These occur most frequently at trick one but, sometimes, they can occur later in the play of the hand also. We will use the club suit as an example but, just in case anyone is wondering, the plays are identical whichever suit is led . . .

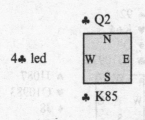

♣ Q2

4♣ led

♣ K85

Against 3NT, West leads a low club. This suggests that he is leading fourth highest, from a long suit headed by an honour card. Should declarer play low from dummy, or should he play the queen?

With only one exception, the correct tactic is to play the honour from the doubleton in dummy. If Q♣ holds the trick, declarer will still have ♣K8 in hand and, provided that East can be kept off lead (he is the danger because he can lead back through the ♣K8 towards West's A♣), that holding still provides a stop. If, instead, declarer leaves the queen in dummy, it will be naked and, whoever holds the ace will wait to gobble that card up later. The singleton queen in dummy will never be a stopper against either opponent.

The situation is identical if it is Kx in dummy and Qxx in hand.

As a general rule, your first thought should be that second hand plays low. However, the beauty (or frustration) of our favourite game is that there are always exceptions to the rules. That is why learning rules is pretty pointless, whereas attempting to understand the situation will reap benefits.

The exception would occur on a hand like this one:

Hand 55   Dealer South

N	E	S	W
–	–	1S	NB
2C	NB	3NT	

```
                    ♠ 92
                    ♥ K64
                    ♦ Q4
                    ♣ AJ10975
   ♠ 543          ┌──────┐        ♠ J1087
   ♥ J7           │   N  │        ♥ Q10983
   ♦ A109532      │ W   E│        ♦ J8
   ♣ 62           │   S  │        ♣ K3
                  └──────┘
                    ♠ AKQ6
                    ♥ A52
                    ♦ K76
                    ♣ Q84
```

West leads 10♦ and declarer realises immediately that the club
suit will be his salvation. However, since the finesse will have to
be taken through West into the East hand, there is no point in
making the usual play of Q♦ from dummy at trick one, since
this leaves ♦K7 in hand, which can be attacked by East if he
were to win with K♣. Therefore, because East will definitely be
the danger hand, declarer should adopt a hold-up approach,
playing low from dummy at trick one and, when East overtakes
with J♦, low from hand also. East will lead back his 8♦, and
declarer plays low from hand again, allowing dummy's Q♦ to
push out West's A♦. Even if West ducks this trick, dummy's Q♦
wins and East is exhausted of diamonds. Now, when South
finesses in clubs and East wins K♣, he cannot return a diamond
and the contract is safe. It is lucky that East only held two
diamonds, but declarer just had to give himself the best chance.

Incidentally, if West holds K♣, it doesn't matter what you do,
since if you finesse West for his king, you will make all six clubs
without losing a trick.

Another situation which causes problems for declarers is this
suit combination:

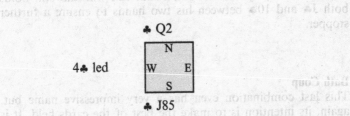

♣ Q2

4♣ led

♣ J85

This time, South's ambition is to take one trick with his holding
in clubs and, to be certain that he succeeds, he must play low
from dummy. This will force East to play A♣ or K♣ to win and
South will still be left with both Q♣ and J♣ to beat the other top
honour – so he must score a trick.

Less experienced players confuse this situation with the previous one and rise with the doubleton honour in dummy. Now,
East may beat Q♣ with a top honour and return a club through
declarer's ♣J8 holding straight into West's strong suit holding.

Here is another position which occurs quite frequently:

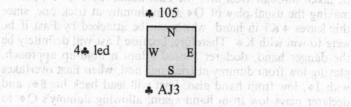

♣ 105

4♣ led

♣ AJ3

All too often declarer is tempted to play 10♣ from dummy. However, when this card gets beaten by an honour in the East hand, if declarer ducks, he then finds that East continues with the suit and South's J♣ gets beaten by West's honour; if South wins with A♣, his ♣J3 is open to devastating attack should East regain the lead.

To ensure two solid stoppers, declarer need only play low from dummy at trick one. If East plays low, South's J♣ wins the trick; if East plays an honour, South can win and still holds both J♣ and 10♣ between his two hands to ensure a further stopper.

Bath Coup

This last combination even has a very impressive name but, again, its intention is to make the best of the cards held. It is quite a common situation and the defence can smoke it out through good technique (see page 167) but it can still make the difference between success and failure.

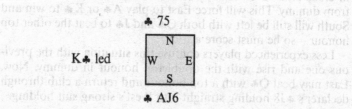

♣ 75

K♣ led

♣ AJ6

When West leads K♣, declarer knows that he also holds ♣Q10, since the lead must be from the top-of-a-broken-sequence (see page 136). To freeze the suit for the opposition, the correct play is to duck, playing 6♣. Now, if West continues leading the suit, South will score both his J♣ and his A♣. If West stops leading the suit and attempts to put his partner on lead to return the suit to him, East-West will have lost the vital tempo required to set up their tricks before South establishes his winners and makes his contract.

On very rare occasions, it may be correct to forgo the Bath Coup and win the first trick. The time when this exception may occur is when, in order to establish your long suit, you will be finessing through the East hand and into the West hand. It is safe to win the first trick in this situation as, if and when West wins a trick, he cannot profitably attack the club suit without providing you with a further trick, sooner or later, with J♣.

These are not situations that you need to memorize, merely to understand as you read them now. Then, take time at the table to assess the situation and play accordingly.

Blockages
A nasty sounding situation which has the potential to crop up frequently and cause you misery. All of us, at some time or another, have found ourselves stranded in the wrong hand, staring longingly at tricks we cannot enjoy, because we are unable to reach our other hand. To ensure that this does not occur, most of the time a simple guideline can be followed:

Aim to play the high card from the shorter holding of the suit.

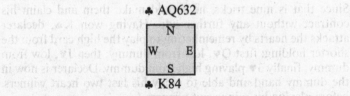

Play K♣ first, then follow with 8♣ to dummy's A♣ and then Q♣. Provided the suit has split reasonably, you will be in the right hand to continue cashing your winners.

The next hand defeated the inexperienced declarer when it was first played:

Hand 56   Dealer South

N	E	S	W
–	–	1D	NB
1H	NB	3NT	

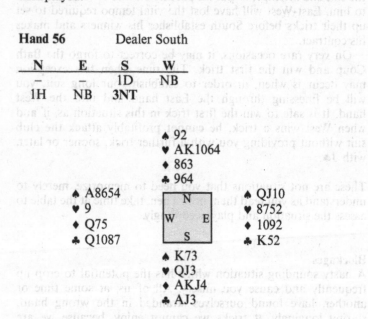

```
                    ♠ 92
                    ♥ AK1064
                    ♦ 863
                    ♣ 964
    ♠ A8654                      ♠ QJ10
    ♥ 9            N             ♥ 8752
    ♦ Q75       W     E          ♦ 1092
    ♣ Q1087        S             ♣ K52
                    ♠ K73
                    ♥ QJ3
                    ♦ AKJ4
                    ♣ AJ3
```

For good players, this hand is a breeze but you need to be careful not to take your eye off the ball at the crucial moment.

When West leads 5♠ and East contributes 10♠, declarer can count one spade trick, five hearts, two diamonds and a club. Since that is nine tricks, he should make them and claim his contract without any further ado. Having won K♠, declarer attacks the hearts by remembering to play the high card from the shorter holding: first Q♥, low from dummy; then J♥, low from dummy; finally 3♥ playing high from dummy. Declarer is now in the dummy hand and able to enjoy his last two heart winners, before playing his minor-suit winners.

This next hand requires far deeper thought to ensure success:

Hand 57   Dealer South

N	E	S	W
–	–	1NT	NB
2NT	NB	3NT	

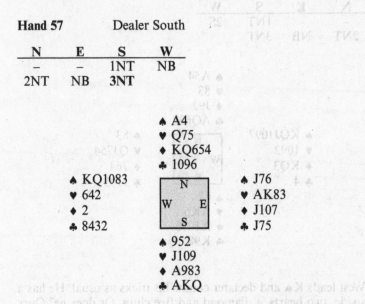

♠ A4
♥ Q75
♦ KQ654
♣ 1096

♠ KQ1083
♥ 642
♦ 2
♣ 8432

♠ J76
♥ AK83
♦ J107
♣ J75

♠ 952
♥ J109
♦ A983
♣ AKQ

West leads K♠ and declarer can see nine tricks for the taking: a spade, five diamonds and three clubs. There is little point holding up A♠ (since you can do it only once anyway) so South takes the trick in dummy and begins to play on diamonds. He must be careful though. He does not want to leave himself with a low card in his hand that is higher than the low cards in dummy, otherwise he will leave his final diamond winner stranded in the entryless dummy. He follows the unblocking guidelines to the full: high card from the shorter holding.

He plays A♦, then 9♦ overtaking with K♦. Now, he plays Q♦ and carefully plays 8♦ from hand. With all the opponents' diamonds played, he can now lead 6♦ from dummy and play his 3♦ beneath it. He is still in dummy to enjoy his 5♦, before cashing his ♣AKQ to claim his contract.

This final hand also concerns awareness of potential blockage, but demands a much more sophisticated solution:

Hand 58   Dealer South

N	E	S	W
–	–	1NT	2S
2NT	NB	3NT	

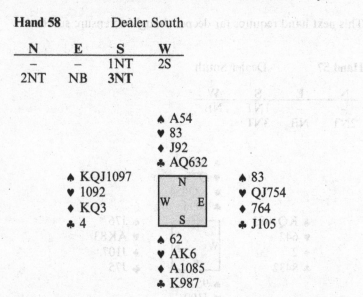

```
              ♠ A54
              ♥ 83
              ♦ J92
              ♣ AQ632
♠ KQJ1097        N          ♠ 83
♥ 1092      W         E     ♥ QJ754
♦ KQ3                       ♦ 764
♣ 4              S          ♣ J105
              ♠ 62
              ♥ AK6
              ♦ A1085
              ♣ K987
```

West leads K♠ and declarer counts his tricks as usual. He has a
spade, two hearts, a diamond and five clubs. Or does he? Once
A♠ is knocked out, he has no entry to dummy, apart from in
clubs and, if you look carefully at the pips of the small cards in
the club suit, you can see that dummy's pips are all smaller than
the declarer's. If he plays K♣, then 9♣ to A♣, cashes Q♣ from
dummy and then 6♣, he will be forced to win in hand with 7♣
and the suit will be blocked, the final club trick stranded in
dummy. Can declarer find a way to unblock the suit?

The key is to realise that declarer must discard a low club from
hand. Thankfully, he is able to hold-up A♠ for two rounds and,
on the third round, win the trick with A♠ and throw away 8♣
from hand. Now, the club suit does not block, and declarer
really can cash his nine tricks.

Counting
Trying to imagine what your opponents hold – or have left in
their hands – is one of the most important, yet difficult parts

of the game. It takes some players years to get there; others even longer. However, the quicker you start to practise, the quicker it will become, if not second nature, then at least not quite as alien as it will feel when you first start putting it into action.

Counting encompasses several different areas:

Counting Points

When your opponents have bid, you should add up the points between you and your partner's hand, subtract that total from 40, and assess how many points each (or both) of your opponents are likely to hold. This alone may allow you to place outstanding cards accurately or, at the very least, appreciate in which hand the high card about which you are concerned is most likely to be located.

Even when your opponents have not bid, you may be able to draw important conclusions. For example, if a hand which did not open the bidding shows up with nine points, then you will know he cannot also hold the ace you are still worrying about.

Counting Distribution

As the subsequent examples will show, especially in NT contracts, the distribution can prove vital to picking both the right line of play and the best form of attack in defence. Choose one opponent's hand to count; this allows deductions about the other hand to be made too.

One of the most important tips in regard to counting is that you should form a picture of how your opponents' hands looked originally. If you try to work out what they have left, the picture changes after every trick and you will find yourself quickly lost. If you are able to form a picture of their original hands, you will find that, almost automatically, you will be able to remember the cards that have been played and, from that, you can deduce what is left in the hand that is concerning you.

Let's see three examples, starting with an apparently hopeless contract:

Hand 59   Dealer South

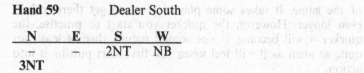

N	E	S	W
–	–	2NT	NB
3NT			

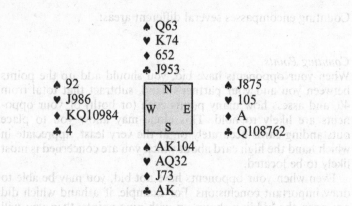

```
                    ♠ Q63
                    ♥ K74
                    ♦ 652
                    ♣ J953
   ♠ 92          ┌──────┐       ♠ J875
   ♥ J986        │  N   │       ♥ 105
   ♦ KQ10984     │W   E │       ♦ A
   ♣ 4           │  S   │       ♣ Q108762
                 └──────┘
                    ♠ AK104
                    ♥ AQ32
                    ♦ J73
                    ♣ AK
```

West led K♦, the suit South was worried about, and the dummy hand did nothing to raise his spirits. South must have thought that he would lose the first five diamond tricks pretty quickly, but it didn't turn out that way. East won with A♦ and then started to think. Declarer realised that East was far too good a player not to return a diamond if he had one, so it seemed that South was going to get a second chance. After some thought, East switched to 10♥ – which cost his side nothing – and South settled down to consider what chances he had.

He had two club, three heart and three spade tricks. He needed one more. If the hearts were split 3–3 or Q♣ fell under ♣AK, that would produce the ninth trick. The spade suit offered two chances: either a 3–3 break, or a finesse against East for J♠. Declarer decided to try all his options whilst carefully tracking the West hand, whom he now knew had started with a 6-card diamond suit.

Declarer won East's 10♥ lead with K♥ in dummy and then cashed ♥AQ in his hand, noting that East showed out on the third round. This meant that his fourth heart was not a winner, but now he knew that West held four hearts as well as six diamonds. Now, South played his ♣AK and West showed out on the second round. Again, this meant that South had not created his ninth trick, but he had learned more about West's hand. Declarer considered what he knew. West had started with four hearts, six diamonds, and one club, and that left only two cards in his hand which could be spades. Declarer's plan was set. He played A♠ from hand and then crossed to dummy with Q♠ – West following with 2♠ and 9♠. This accounted for all West's cards so, when declarer led dummy's last spade and East played low, South played 10♠ from hand, knowing that West would have no more and that 10♠ would be his extra trick. Sure enough, West showed out and declarer claimed his K♠ and his contract.

There was no point in declarer worrying about both opponents' hands. He concentrated on one of them and was able to extrapolate all the distributional information he required for success.

This type of hand takes strong concentration but no particular skills, other then the ability to count to thirteen. The next time suits start splitting badly for you, take time to analyse whether the bad news can be turned to good effect by considering the implications of the distribution.

On the next deal, an opponent has bid and that provides the clue for the winning line.

Hand 60   Dealer East

N	E	S	W
–	1H	1NT	NB
3NT			

When West leads J♥, South immediately counts the number of points between his hand and dummy, which is always a good move when you are playing a hand after an opponent has opened the bidding or competed in the auction. He finds that North-South hold 27 points between them, leaving East-West with 13. Since West has led a jack, that leaves only 12 points and it seems likely that East holds them all. That means that declarer can finesse East for Q♣, but the diamond finesse looks doomed. Since South needs two diamond tricks without losing the lead more than once, he seems to be in a pickle. However, now that he has told himself that East must hold K♦ for his opening bid, at least he can reject the diamond finesse as pointless.

Hand 60   *Dealer East*

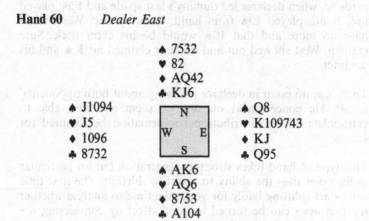

♠ 7532
♥ 82
♦ AQ42
♣ KJ6

♠ J1094
♥ J5
♦ 1096
♣ 8732

♠ Q8
♥ K109743
♦ KJ
♣ Q95

♠ AK6
♥ AQ6
♦ 8753
♣ A104

Declarer wins J♥ lead with Q♥ in hand and crosses to dummy with K♣. He leads J♣ and East covers with Q♣, allowing South to win with A♣. His 10♣ is a winner which he can save until later. Now, he must turn his attention to diamonds. Declarer's best hope is that East holds a singleton or doubleton diamond and, to this end, he plays a low diamond to dummy's ace, and watches East's J♦ fall. Now, he plays a low diamond from dummy and East's king pops up. East returns a heart, but South wins, plays a diamond to dummy's queen, cashes the final diamond and then returns to hand to enjoy his three black-suit winners.

The key to success was the simple realisation that the diamond finesse could not be the winning play.

Finally, in this section, a matter of distribution for declarer to consider – and at a high level.

Hand 61   Dealer South

N	E	S	W
–	–	2NT	NB
7NT			

If only auctions were that simple in real life. However, North's bid is perfectly decent, as is the contract. Can South bring home the grand slam?

West leads 10♠ and South reflects that he will have to locate the position of Q♣ to succeed.

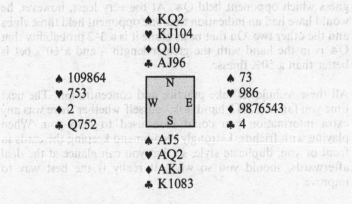

♠ KQ2
♥ KJ104
♦ Q10
♣ AJ96

♠ 109864   ♠ 73
♥ 753   ♥ 986
♦ 2   ♦ 9876543
♣ Q752   ♣ 4

♠ AJ5
♥ AQ2
♦ AKJ
♣ K1083

With no bidding to guide him, only the distribution can help, so he begins to play out all his spades, hearts and diamonds and he keeps a concentrated eye on one of his opponents' hands. Since West has led, he watches his hand.

When South plays all three spade tricks, he sees that East shows out after two rounds, marking West with five spades. Next, South plays his four heart winners, and East and West both follow to three rounds; East throwing a diamond on the fourth round and South and West a low club. Declarer now knows eight of West's cards. When South plays his three diamond winners, West shows out on the second round, marking him with just one diamond. South does some addition: West held five spades, plus three hearts, plus one diamond. That makes nine cards accounted for. West's last four cards must be clubs. Since North-South hold eight clubs and West four, East is marked with only one club. Now, declarer can see his way home. He leads K♣ from hand and watches East produce 4♣ – he did this in case East's singleton club was the queen. However, 4♣ is East's last club so the finesse against West is indicated. South leads 8♣ and when West plays low – trying to look nonchalant no doubt – declarer plays J♣ from dummy and it holds the trick. Dummy's A♣ is the thirteenth club and the contract is home.

Of course, the uneven distribution in East and West's hands helped the declarer enormously. If East and West had followed to all the spades, hearts and diamonds, South would have had to guess which opponent held Q♣. At the very least, however, he would have had an indication that one opponent held three clubs and the other two. On that basis alone it is a 3–2 probability that Q♣ is in the hand with the greater length – and a 60% bet is better than a 50% finesse.

All these techniques take practice and concentration. The next time you fail in a 3NT hand, ask yourself whether there was any extra information you could have used to help you. When playing with friends, I strongly recommend keeping the cards in front of you, duplicate style, so that you can glance at the deal afterwards, should you so wish. It really is the best way to improve.

6

NO-TRUMP CONTRACTS –
FOCUS ON DEFENCE

No-trump contracts should be attacked! Unlike suit contracts on which the auction will largely determine the defence strategy, a fairly aggressive stance can be taken against all NT contracts. This is because there is less subtlety when defending NTs – and more of a hurry to take your tricks. Simply, a NT contract is a race between declarer and defence to see who can establish their long suit (or suits) first. The defenders have the advantage that they get to lead their long suit first; the declarer that he can see both his side's hands. If the defence switch from their first suit to another this squanders their advantage so, unless you know that it is completely wrong, you should continue to play on the suit led originally, even if it means losing the lead several times. Eventually, you will establish your suit and, if you can regain the lead elsewhere, you will then be able to cash your winners. NT contracts are rarely defeated by switching from one suit to another in an attempt to pick off tricks. Occasionally, at Duplicate bridge – where your aim is to limit the tricks taken by declarer, but not necessarily to beat the contract – careful, passive defence may be right. At Rubber bridge, Chicago and Teams of Four you must try to defeat the contract so passive defence is almost never right.

As with the defence against suit contracts, defenders must communicate information to one another through their leads, the cards they play in that suit subsequently, and also through signals and discards. Even if you find interpreting this information too difficult for now, practise making the correct plays so that you and your partner can gently work towards a better understanding of what is happening in all four hands. Then, you will be in a position to create inspirational plays that will amaze and deflate your opponents.

Leads
Your general policy will be to lead your longest suit unless it has been bid by the opposition. Importantly, you must have some form of re-entry to your hand so that, once your tricks are established, you can regain the lead in order to enjoy them.

If you hold a very weak hand and you feel that you are unlikely to win any trick during the play, it will be better to try to lead your partner's long suit since, if you are so weak, your partner will be stronger and is therefore likely to have outside entries with which to gain the lead and cash winners in his long suit. Obviously, you may have to guess which suit will be your partner's longest but sometimes the auction or even a lead-directing double (see page 179) will guide you. Even so, be prepared to make the odd embarrassing error in your attempts to be a hero.

Lead Styles
Your style of lead will be the same as against suit contracts with the additional freedom that you can lead away from an ace, since it is the length of your suit which is its strongest asset and which takes priority over safety considerations. Once you have chosen which suit you should lead, the top-of-a-sequence of honours, or of a broken or an internal sequence, still takes priority over fourth highest because a top-of-sequence lead combines both attack and safety. Let's review the lead styles:

Top-of-a-Sequence and Broken Sequence
With its combined safety and attack profile, this should be your favourite lead. Against suit contracts, you might decide to lead from just two honour cards in a row, whereas against no-trumps you need three cards involved. The lowest sequence is 1098, the lowest broken sequence 1097. Lower sequences should merely be viewed as low cards.

These can be led against NT contracts

KQJx   KQ10x   QJ10x   QJ9x   J109xx   1097x

Internal Sequence
This is a sequence inside a suit – with a higher card above the sequence. Against a suit contract, you would not lead an internal sequence from a suit headed by the ace – you would not lead that suit at all. Against NTs, it does not matter so much giving away a quick trick if your suit becomes established in the long run, so leading from a suit headed by an ace is perfectly acceptable. Your partner may not be certain whether your lead is top-of-a-sequence or top-of-an-internal-sequence but, usually, his own hand and dummy will reveal the truth.

KJ109x   Q109xx   AJ10xx   AQJxx   A1097x

Leading from an Honour
A key understanding of basic card-play is that leads of low cards indicate an interest in your partner winning the trick and returning the suit to you as soon as possible. This is because the lead of a low card indicates that you hold an honour card or cards at the head of the suit. The standard lead is "fourth highest"; when you hold only three cards, it should be the bottom one.

Against NT contracts leading from a suit headed by an ace is quite acceptable, even desirable

KJxx   Axxxx   AJxxx   Q10xxx   Kxx   Q10xx   J10xx

Top-of-Rubbish
If a low intermediate card indicates interest in the suit, then when you hold no honour cards in the suit you have decided to lead, you must lead a high card to indicate to partner your lack of interest in the suit. Usually, this will be the second highest or, if that card seems low, lead your highest card to make the message as clear as possible.

9752   10852   8432   987   98765

Notice that 10s, without the 9 or a higher honour, are not honour cards and that sequences below 1097 are not regarded as important enough to indicate.

Assuming the auction 1NT – 3NT from your opponents, let's take a look at some good leads:

♠ A65   The best lead here is K♦ – top-of-a-sequence
♥ 86   – since you can continue to play diamonds
♦ KQJ102   until A♦ is dislodged and then, when you
♣ 754   regain the lead with A♠, you can cash your
               remaining diamond winners. By the time you
               have played four rounds of diamonds, even
               your little 2♦ will be a winner and may be the
               card that defeats the contract.

♠ A954   Here, Q♥ looks best. A low spade is possible
♥ QJ96   but with equal length in both majors, the
♦ 73   top-of-a-broken-sequence takes priority since
♣ 874   it is safer and requires less from your partner
               to make the lead work well. You are hoping
               that your partner holds either a top heart or
               another outside entry so that both A♥ and
               K♥ can be dislodged to establish two tricks
               for your side.

♠ AJ1074   When you hold three honours at the head of
♥ 42   your chosen suit, you must lead an honour.
♦ Q953   Here, J♠ is top-of-an-internal-sequence. If
♣ 76   your partner does not hold a top spade then
               J♠ will push out one honour from your
               opponents and you may be able to capture the
               other with your A♠ later.

Leading from a suit headed by ace-queen-ten is slightly different from usual as you will observe in the two examples below:

♠ AQ1053
♥ 65
♦ 853
♣ 973

Even though you hold no sequence, because you have three honours, you should lead an honour card. Since your A♠ is your re-entry to your hand, you should choose Q♠ as your lead. If your partner holds J♠ or K♠, he will usually play it (see page 150) or, without an honour card, he will show you his count in the suit, so that you can judge which card to lead next.

♠ AQ1053
♥ 65
♦ 853
♣ A73

This time, you do hold an outside entry, A♣, so you can afford to lead A♠ to see dummy before deciding with which card to continue. Again, partner will jettison any honour card he holds (see page 152) or show the number of cards he holds in the suit by way of a count signal (see page 99). You will then be able to assess how best to continue the suit or, on rare occasions, opt for a switch.

♠ AJ642
♥ AJ7
♦ 8642
♣ 5

With no sequence, fourth highest is the lead. The lead of a low card indicates an honour, or broken honours, at the head of the suit, and asks partner to try to win the trick and return the suit to you immediately and subsequently.

♠ 98642
♥ A53
♦ A42
♣ K7

With so many outside entries, it is still worth leading your long suit, despite its poor quality. Even if you have to push out three stoppers from your opponents' hands, you will set up two tricks for yourself and you have the chance of regaining the lead three times. By leading a high card, you indicate that your suit is poor quality, since a fourth highest lead guarantees at least one honour card at the head of the suit. A ten on its own is not an honour and you should usually lead second highest from these poor suit holdings.

♠ 97532 Since you have such a poor hand, it will be
♥ J105   better to try to lead your partner's long suit. It
♦ 864   is a guess, but as your opponents have not
♣ 93   used Stayman, dummy is unlikely to contain a
          4-card major suit. Therefore a major suit lead
          sounds good. J♥ might hit partner's 4- or
          5-card suit and, if it does, he will have the
          necessary high cards to act as re-entries.

Leading against a NT contract when you hold AK at the head of
your suit is an art in itself and should be discussed with a regular
partner before play. However, the methods below are widely
played:

♠ AK4   Since you have no long suit from which to lead
♥ 753   you try A♠ to have a look at dummy and to
♦ 6532   see partner's response to your lead. The lead
♣ 963   of an ace against a NT contract specifically
          shows this holding (unless you are leading
          your partner's bid suit when it indicates an ace
          doubleton – or possibly singleton). If partner
          holds the Q♠ or four cards or more in spades,
          he will play the highest card he can afford by
          way of an encouraging Attitude Signal (see
          page 91). If he is short in spades, he will make
          a discouraging discard by playing his lowest
          card. You will then switch to another suit
          having been able to view dummy whilst
          retaining the lead.

♠ AKJ75 When you hold length in a suit headed by
♥ 64   AKJ you should lead the king. This is the one
♦ 984   time you do not lead the top-of-a-sequence.
♣ 853   Partner will jettison Q♠ if he holds it, or he
          will show how many cards he holds in the suit,
          so that you can judge how to continue. (See
          page 99 for full details.)

How your partner deals with each of these leads is vital to the success of your strategy. In the next section, we will ensure that the play of the suit runs smoothly and offers your side the best chance of a successful attack against declarer.

Leading Partner's Suit

In the old days, the common agreement was always to lead the top card you held in your partner's suit. Whilst this is, on very rare occasions right, it is far more often likely to give away extra tricks to declarer. When leading your partner's bid suit, generally you should follow the standard rules of leading against no-trumps, with the one exception that with any two touching honours you should always lead the higher – you no longer need three cards involved for the sequence to be valid.

Since you would always lead the higher of two cards in your partner's suit, and the top of any touching honours, the one time you might be faced with a tough decision is when you hold three or four cards headed by an honour. Now, you should usually lead your little card (indicating an honour at the head of the suit). This is so your honour can still beat a lower honour which the declarer may hold.

Hand 62   **Dealer North**

N	E	S	W
1D	1S	2NT	NB
3NT			

When this hand was first played, West was of the old school, who always led the highest card in his partner's suit. He led Q♠ and East played low, allowing South to win with his K♠. Declarer immediately attacked diamonds, finessing to East, who took the trick with his K♦. East returned A♠ with then 9♠ which declarer won with his jack. Now, declarer could cash four diamond tricks and three club tricks to go with his two spades and the contract was made.

Hand 62   *Dealer North*

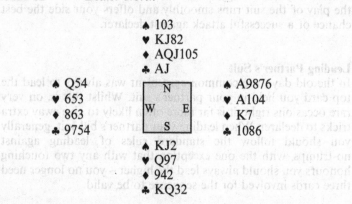

```
              ♠ 103
              ♥ KJ82
              ♦ AQJ105
              ♣ AJ
  ♠ Q54          N          ♠ A9876
  ♥ 653     W       E       ♥ A104
  ♦ 863          S          ♦ K7
  ♣ 9754                    ♣ 1086
              ♠ KJ2
              ♥ Q97
              ♦ 942
              ♣ KQ32
```

If the correct procedure were to be followed, the defence would run far more smoothly. West would lead 4♠ – a low card indicating an honour at the head of the suit – and East would win with A♠ before returning 7♠. South would do best now to rise with K♠ to block the suit and leave West with the bare queen but, even if he did this, he would probably still be a trick short. If South played low on this spade return, West would win with Q♠, play his final spade to clear the suit and, when East cashed his K♦, he would have two further spade winners to cash, plus his A♥, and the contract would fail by two tricks. The key is that South's 2NT response indicated spade stops and West should therefore keep his Q♠ over South so as to take one of his honours. By denying him a second spade stopper, he saves both a trick, and improves the timing of the defence.

The one time it might be right to lead the top card in partner's bid suit is when you suspect, from the auction, that the stoppers in the suit are likely to be in dummy and by leading a high card you will push one of those stoppers towards your partner's good holding. However, since it will be the NT bidder who likely holds the stoppers, this situation occurs very infrequently.

MUD

Incidentally, to indicate three low cards (not including jack, queen, king, or ace) you should lead your middle card. This is known as MUD. This stands for Middle – Up – Down, and shows that from three small cards you are playing your middle card then, when next following to the suit, you will play your top card and finally your bottom card.

Partner's Reaction to 4th Highest Lead

If you lead a low card, your partner should try to win the trick and return the suit to you. There are a number of situations which occur routinely at trick one and which can have a profound effect on the whole deal. Once you learn to recognise them and tune your reactions, both you and your partner will begin to be able to interpret the information available and put it to devastating effect against your opponents. Above all, you must always take time to interpret your partner's lead and try to visualize his hand. Then, even complicated plays may seem obvious to you. Let's take a look at these key plays:

1.   Try to win the trick by playing the lowest of touching cards:

When you lead, you play the top-of-a-sequence of high cards; when receiving a lead from your partner (or if dummy or declarer leads the suit) you should play the lower/lowest of touching cards.

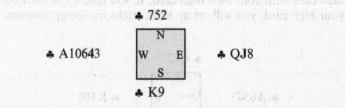

♣ 752

♣ A10643   ♣ QJ8

♣ K9

If partner leads 4♣ and dummy plays low, you should play J♣. When declarer wins this trick with K♣, partner will then suspect that you hold Q♣ also. (He cannot know for sure, since the declarer could hold both K♣ and Q♣ and choose to win the trick with K♣ to deceive the defence.) If you play Q♣, you definitely deny that you hold J♣.

2. If dummy fails to play an honour, try to win the trick with the lowest card that will do the job:

Whilst this is obvious advice, sometimes less experienced players forget that once dummy has failed to play an honour to the trick, that card is now out of play for that trick.

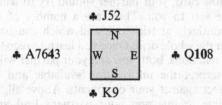

If partner leads 4♣ and dummy plays low, you should try to win the trick with 10♣, since J♣ is now out of the trick. This will force declarer to win with K♣ and partner will suspect that you hold Q♣. If you play Q♣, not only will this deny 10♣, but it will set up J♣ in dummy as a certain second stopper.

3. If dummy fails to play an honour, save your honour for that card later and try to win the trick with a lower card:

This is good card-play practice: you want to take an opponent's high card with your own high card. If you take a low card with your high card, you will set up extra tricks for the opposition.

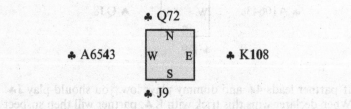

Here, when declarer plays 2♣ from dummy, you should play your 10♣, saving your K♣ for dummy's Q♣ later. In this instance, your play forces declarer to win the trick now – or he

will make none in clubs at all – and you will still have clubs left
to return to your partner if you gain the lead later.

There is a still greater advantage when the layout is like this:

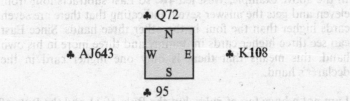

♣ Q72

♣ AJ643

♣ K108

♣ 95

Now, your 10♣ wins the trick and you can return K♣ (leading
the higher of two cards as always) and then 8♣ to partner's ace,
and you take the first five tricks. How likely is it that declarer
will have such poor clubs? Well, we would all like brilliant
stoppers in every suit when we play NTs, but often that isn't
possible.

This situation can occur with even smaller cards:

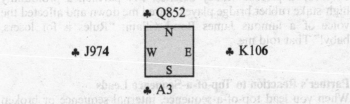

♣ Q852

♣ J974

♣ K106

♣ A3

When partner leads 4♣, if dummy plays low, you should insert
6♣! This pushes out declarer's A♣ and allows you to lie in wait
with ♣K10 over dummy's ♣Q85. Declarer is now unlikely to be
able to have time to establish Q♣ as another trick.

How could East know that playing 6♣ would be sufficient to
push out a high card from South? He applies the Rule of 11.

Rule of 11
Assuming that your partner has led fourth highest, the Rule of
11 states that:

If you subtract from 11 the value (number) of the card led, the answer will indicate the number of cards higher than that located in the other three hands.

In the above example, West led 4♣, so East subtracts four from eleven and gets the answer seven, indicating that there are seven cards higher than the four in the other three hands. Since East can see three higher cards in dummy and three more in his own hand, this means that there is only one higher card in the declarer's hand.

I am not a huge fan of rules, but the Rule of 11 and the Rule of 7 (see page 107) are two of the best. The Rule of 11 can also be applied by the declarer to discover useful information but, often, there are more important things to consider (such as why the defender has chosen to lead one suit over another). So, bear them in mind, but do not become hide-bound by any of these rules – or any others you may pick up, or be lectured on by "helpful" opponents, elderly relatives, or club "experts". This game is about logical thought, and the understanding of why things happen. I once quoted the Rule of 11 in an attempt to cover up a piece of lousy defence. My partner, a profoundly high-stake rubber bridge player, stared me down and affected the voice of a famous James Bond villain: "Rules is for losers, baby!" That told me.

Partner's Reaction to Top-of-a-Sequence Leads
When you lead top-of-a-sequence, internal sequence or broken sequence, there are some specific rules which partner should follow to ensure that the best is made of what is, already, a promising situation. Above all, partner needs to inform you about the location of the remaining high cards, and to get out of your way to ensure that there is no blockage.

With only very few exceptions, the underlying rule is as follows:

If partner leads an honour card against a NT contract, you should play any honour card you hold immediately.

We will take a look at the exceptions after each example, but they are rare whereas the main situation occurs frequently:

1. Overtake to unblock:

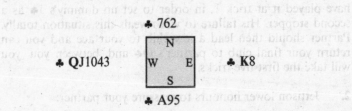

When partner leads Q♣, his lead must be from either ♣QJ10 or ♣QJ9. If you play low on partner's Q♣, you will be left with the singleton king. If declarer ducks and partner leads another club, you may win with your K♣, but you will have no further clubs to lead and your attack on that suit will be over. If, instead, you overtake your partner's queen with your king and then return the suit, your partner can continue to lead clubs until declarer's A♣ is dislodged and then, if partner regains the lead, he can cash his remaining winners in the suit. In effect, this is just playing a high card from the shorter holding, just as you would do if you were the declarer playing the suit between your own hand and dummy. You would make the same play if you held ♣K82, returning 8♣ if declarer ducked the first trick (see page 154).

The sole exception would occur when you held three cards and dummy held the missing honour if, by overtaking, you were to promote that card into a winner:

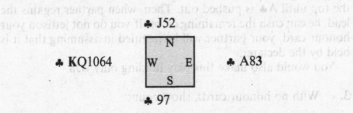

Here, if you overtake partner's K♣ with your ace, you promote dummy's J♣ into a third round winner. Instead, play low on partner's lead. When partner's K♣ holds the trick he will deduce that you must hold A♣ since, if declarer held it, he would surely have played it at trick 1, in order to set up dummy's J♣ as a second stopper. His failure to win reveals this situation totally. Partner should then lead a low club to your ace and you can return your final club to partner's Q♣ and, between you, you will take the first five tricks.

2.   Jettison lower honours to reassure your partner:

When partner leads top-of-a-broken-sequence, he will, as well as worrying about where the top honour(s) lies, also wonder where the missing honour in his broken sequence is placed. If you hold it, play it at once to reassure your partner that he can continue to lead his suit.

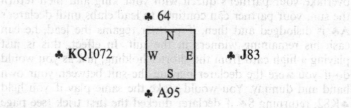

When partner leads K♣ and you hold J♣, you know that he must be leading from ♣KQ10. If you had held A♣ you would have played it. Here you cannot do that but you do have a chance to show your partner that you, not the declarer, hold J♣. By playing J♣, partner can now continue to lead his suit from the top until A♣ is pushed out. Then, when partner regains the lead, he can cash the remaining clubs. If you do not jettison your honour card, your partner will be justified in assuming that it is held by the declarer.

You would also make this play holding only ♣J8.

3.   With no honour cards, show count:

When you hold no honour cards in the suit led by your partner, your duty is to indicate how many cards you hold in the suit, so that partner can decide how best to continue. You achieve this by playing a card from your hand in accordance with your count signals (page 99) which are, basically, a high card to show an even number of cards, a low card to show an odd number of cards. From the auction, the look of dummy and his own hand, partner will usually be able to work out how many cards you hold and, therefore, how many are held by the declarer.

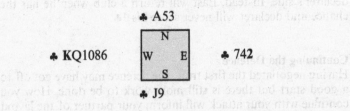

♣ A53

♣ KQ1086   ♣ 742

♣ J9

Partner leads K♣, dummy plays low and, with no honour to play, East shows count by playing a low card. Now, partner must count out the suit. West holds five clubs, dummy three and East appears to hold three cards as well. (East could hold only one club, but declarer might have won the first trick with dummy's A♣ if that had been the case.) West can therefore conclude that declarer started with only two clubs and that he now holds a singleton J♣. West can continue with Q♣, pinning declarer's J♣ and ensuring that the suit is established with the loss of only one trick.

The count signal can also warn off your partner from continuing when it is wrong to do so:

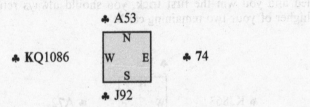

♣ A53

♣ KQ1086   ♣ 74

♣ J92

When West leads K♣, East shows count by playing 7♣ – his highest card – indicating an even number of cards. East should do this whether or not dummy has played A♣. This confirms that he does not hold J♣ – since he would have jettisoned it whether or not dummy played his A♣ – and that he holds two cards in the suit. West can work out that he cannot hold four cards, since declarer would then be left with a singleton J♣ and it would have appeared on the first trick. When West has a chance to lead clubs again, he will reject it, realising that by leading the suit from his side of the table, he will set up an extra trick for the declarer's side. Instead, East will return a club when he has the chance and declarer will never score his J♣.

Continuing the Defence
Having negotiated the first trick, the defence may have got off to a good start but there is still more work to be done. How you continue with your attack will inform your partner of the layout of the suit for him to appreciate what needs to be done – and what needs to be left well alone.

Returning Partner's Suit
Having won trick one, which card do you return? Partner will be delighted that you have won the suit that he has led, but he will be watching which card you return so that he can visualize the layout of the suit. To this end, there are some basic rules to be followed:

1.   Always return the higher of two cards:

When you started with three cards in the suit your partner has led and you win the first trick, you should always return the higher of your two remaining cards.

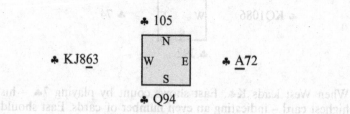

♣ 105

♣ KJ86<u>3</u>   ♣ <u>A</u>72

Here, East takes partner's 6♣ lead with his ace, and then returns the higher of his two remaining cards – 7♣. When South plays 9♣ and partner wins with J♣, he will wonder whether declarer has just Q♣ left or whether he holds ♣Q2. If it is the former holding, he will want to lay down his K♣ and then cash his two further winners; if it is the latter holding, he may leave clubs alone to avoid setting up Q♣ for the declarer.

In this example, West will notice that 2♣ has not been played by East or the declarer and will deduce that East probably holds it, and that South therefore now holds only the singleton Q♣. When he lays down K♣, all is revealed, and the defence have taken the first five tricks.

If, on the other hand, this were the layout, West would know better than to continue leading his suit:

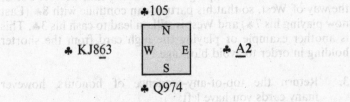

♣105

♣ KJ863   ♣ A2

♣ Q974

When East wins trick one with A♣ and then returns 2♣, West will know that, as Q♣ has not appeared from the declarer, East held only two clubs and the declarer four. To cash his K♣ now would establish declarer's Q♣ as a trick. Although West may choose to do this – perhaps because he knows he will regain the lead later and his final club will set the contract – he may decide that he would rather not provide a trick for the declarer and instead switch to a different suit.

2.   Return the lowest of three cards:

When you start with four cards in the suit your partner has led, you can be certain that you have got off to the best possible start. Having won trick one, return the lowest of your three remaining cards.

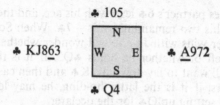

Here, having taken trick one with A♣, East returns his lowest card from his three remaining cards. Although this is the same card as in the above example, this time South plays Q♣ – something he would not do if he held four cards headed by the queen – and so West will know that this is his last card and West can win with his K♣ and continue leading his suit.

Incidentally, when West does continue leading clubs by playing his J♣, East should play the higher of his two remaining cards on this trick, dropping 9♣. By doing this, he gets out of the way of West, so that his partner can continue with 8♣ (East now playing his 7♣) and West is still on lead to cash his 3♣. This is another example of playing the high card from the shorter holding in order to avoid blockage.

3.   Return the top-of-any-sequence of honours, however many cards you have left:

If you have a sequence of honour cards, even just two, you should play the top-of-your-sequence.

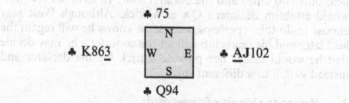

When West leads 3♣ and East wins with A♣, East should return J♣ (and not the lowest of his remaining cards), since top-of-a-sequence always take priority. Here, it is essential since, if East had returned 2♣, declarer could have played 9♣ and this would have forced out West's K♣, establishing Q♣ for the declarer. As it is, when East returns J♣, declarer's Q♣ is caught in the trap between East's card and his partner's king and East-West will take the first four tricks without breaking sweat.

East would also return J♣ if he had started with just ♣AJ10.

Any sequence of cards smaller than J10 does not count as a sequence and the cards should be treated as small cards.

4.   If, by trick two, dummy is void in the suit led, always return the highest of your remaining cards:

This is important advice since it will inform your partner of the position of the remaining high cards and allow him to judge how best to continue to attack the suit. It will also ensure that any high card(s) that declarer holds will be pushed into the waiting jaws of your partner's holding.

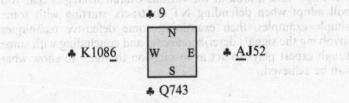

```
            ♣ 9
          N
♣ K1086  W   E  ♣ AJ52
          S
          ♣ Q743
```

When West leads 6♣ and East wins with A♣, he sees that dummy is now void, so he must return the highest (or higher) of his remaining cards. By leading J♣, declarer is placed in an unbearable situation: if he plays low, East retains the lead and can lead 5♣ (always leading the higher card from two) pushing declarer's Q♣ into the jaws of West's ♣K10; if declarer covers J♣ with Q♣, West can win with K♣ and then cash his two further club winners, to take the first four tricks.

Notice that, if East had merely returned the lowest of his three remaining cards – 2♣ – declarer could cover with his 4♣ and West would have to win with 8♣. He could not now continue to lead the suit without setting up declarer's queen. Instead, he would have to wait until East regained the lead (if he does) before East could lead clubs through the declarer's holding once more. That would be poor timing and might well result in declarer triumphing.

That, you may be pleased to know, is the end of the technical card combinations. They are complicated but they need not be learnt by rote. Between you and your partner (or within your group of friends) you will be able to practise these techniques until they become second nature. Because they occur on every hand you defend, they are easy to practise and will soon be assimilated into your bank of knowledge. Slowly, as you begin to use the information provided, you will gain insights into the distribution and placement of the high cards which will enhance your defence enormously. As you begin to defeat more and more of your opponents' contracts, you will get the impression that your cards are improving. Your opponents will lose confidence whilst you gain it, and the positive spiral will begin to improve your results throughout your game.

Let's now take a look at the various overall strategies that you will adopt when defending NT contracts, starting with some simple examples, then examining some defensive techniques involving the signals described above, and concluding with some tough expert plays to act as inspiration to you – to show what can be achieved.

Attack One Suit Only
Unless you are certain that it is hopeless to continue playing the suit led originally, you should pursue it, even if this means relinquishing the lead. For example:

Hand 63   Dealer East

N	E	S	W	
–	1H	1NT†	NB	† 16–18pts
3NT				

Hand 63   *Dealer East*

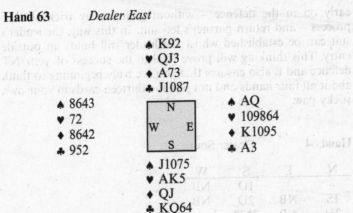

```
                    ♠ K92
                    ♥ QJ3
                    ♦ A73
                    ♣ J1087
    ♠ 8643                          ♠ AQ
    ♥ 72          ┌─────────┐       ♥ 109864
    ♦ 8642        │ N       │       ♦ K1095
    ♣ 952       W │       E │       ♣ A3
                  │    S    │
                  └─────────┘
                    ♠ J1075
                    ♥ AK5
                    ♦ QJ
                    ♣ KQ64
```

West leads the suit his partner called. This is correct, even though South has indicated two stoppers in East's suit by overcalling 1NT. Only if you think that your suit truly offers a better chance than your partner's would you not lead his suit. Since West has a hand that could not conceivably be better than anything his partner may have, he makes his one and only positive contribution to the defence by leading 7♥ – the higher of a 2-card suit. Declarer plays low from dummy, East puts in 8♥ (the lowest of touching cards) and South wins with K♥. Declarer now plays a low club to dummy's jack and East wins with his A♣. Despite the fact that East realises that declarer must hold A♥ and he can see ♥QJ in dummy, he should continue to attack hearts and not contemplate switching to his other suit, diamonds. So, East plays 10♥ and declarer wins in dummy with the jack. Declarer returns to hand with a club and leads J♠, hoping to find West with the queen. When he runs this card to East, East takes it with his Q♠ and plays another heart, causing South's ace and dummy's queen to crash on one another. Now, when East regains the lead with either A♠ or K♦, he has two further hearts to cash and the contract is scuppered.

The Partner of the Leader's Responsibilities
The partner of the leader against NT contracts should be very clear where his responsibilities lie. His duty is to win a trick

early on in the defence – without giving away tricks in the process – and return partner's led suit. In this way, the leader's suit can be established whilst the leader still holds an outside entry. This thinking will prove vital to the success of your NT defence and it also ensures that you are truly beginning to think about all four hands and not just the thirteen cards in your own sticky paw.

Hand 64   Dealer South

N	E	S	W
–	–	1D	NB
1S	NB	2D	NB
2H	NB	3NT	

♠ AKJ74
♥ KQ104
♦ 103
♣ 97

♠ 982   ♠ Q1063
♥ 732   ♥ 986
♦ K6   ♦ A72
♣ KJ1084   ♣ 532

♠ 5
♥ AJ5
♦ QJ9854
♣ AQ6

This deal illustrates the need for both defenders to focus on the real crux of the hand: getting their side's suit established before declarer gets his suit set up.

West led J♣. Declarer realised that he would have to lose the lead twice in diamonds to establish the suit, or risk a spade finesse, which he would prefer to avoid. To this end, declarer ducked the first trick and, when West led 10♣, South won with the queen. Declarer crossed to dummy by playing a low heart to the king, and then he played 10♦. East, with his poor hand, was snoozing quietly and contributed 2♦. West took this trick with his K♦ reluctantly (since it was his last outside entry) and led another club. South won this and played another diamond, hoping that East held the ace. When East took this, he had no clubs left to lead, and now declarer could win whatever was returned and claim the rest of the tricks.

If East had been focused on his responsibilities, the defence would have been a great deal more successful – a whole three tricks more successful. When declarer leads a diamond from dummy, East should rise with A♦ and lead back his last club. Now, West's last two clubs are established and, when he regains the lead with K♦, he can cash his winners to defeat the contract.

Notice that the declarer tried to make it as hard as possible for East to make the right play. Had South lazily led a diamond from hand, it would have been relatively easy for West to play low and East would have won with his ace and returned his club. By crossing to dummy and making East play second, at least declarer tested East's concentration. On this occasion, he found it wanting and made the contract as a result.

Keep the key defensive thoughts to the forefront of your mind at all times and you are far more likely to succeed:

1. You are trying to establish your side's long suit before declarer establishes his suit.
2. The leader's partner should try to win a trick in an outside suit first, return partner's lead, and hope that the leader can then regain the lead to cash his winners.
3. Defending NTs is a key time when the guideline "second hand plays low" may not be appropriate. (See page 101.)

Covering Honours with Honours
The old adage for defenders, "cover an honour with an honour", is a good one, but it should not be obeyed blindly. As with all so-called rules, it is important to understand why you are taking the action, so that you can then judge when it is the best play and when it should be avoided.

The principle is that by playing an honour card on top of your opponent's honour card, you force out a second high card from your opponent and, in the process, promote lower cards into winners, hopefully for a member of your side. Let's see this in action:

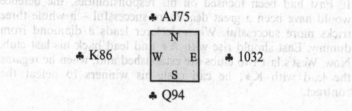

♣ AJ75

♣ K86   ♣ 1032

♣ Q94

South leads Q♣. If West plays low, dummy also plays low and the queen holds the trick. South then leads a low club, West plays low again and dummy plays J♣, which holds the trick. Now, A♣ is cashed, felling both West's K♣ and East's 10♣. The defence have made no tricks.

If, instead, West covers South's Q♣ with his K♣, dummy must play A♣ – this has used two of North-South's honours to win the trick. When J♣ is cashed, everyone follows low and, now, East's 10♣ has been promoted into a card that will win the third round of the suit.

So, the first principle to be followed is that you should:

Cover an honour with an honour if you cannot see the two cards directly below the one led.

In this way, your partner (or you) may hold one of these cards and it will be promoted into a card of trick-taking value.

What should you do if you can see two touching honour cards and one is led?

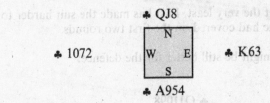

♣ QJ8

♣ 1072 ♣ K63

♣ A954

Dummy leads Q♣; East should play low and plan to cover J♣ when that card is led. By covering J♣, South will have to play A♣ and West's 10♣ will take the third round of the suit.

If, incorrectly, East covers Q♣ when it is led, declarer will win with A♣ and could then lead a low club from hand and, when West plays low, finesse against him for 10♣, by playing dummy's 8♣. This would win, and the suit would be brought in without loss.

So, principle number two is:

If you can see two or more touching honour cards in dummy, you should only cover the last of those cards to be led.

The final principle can prove very important and is often overlooked because the defender becomes disheartened by a gloomy situation.

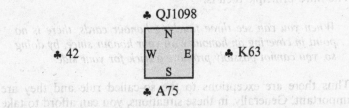

♣ QJ1098

♣ 42 ♣ K63

♣ A75

Dummy leads Q♣ and, following the above principle, East should not play his king. When J♣ is led, East should still not play his king. On the third round, when 10♣ is led, East has to play his king and South wins with his ace. However, he has now run out of clubs and, unless he has an entry to dummy, ♣98 will be stranded. At the very least, East has made the suit harder to enjoy than if he had covered on the first two rounds.

The situation might be still better for the defence:

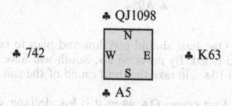

♣ QJ1098

♣ 742   ♣ K63

♣ A5

Declarer might well try leading Q♣ in the hope that a lazy East will cover. When East does not cover, declarer will have to play another club to his A♣, then return to dummy to dislodge East's K♣ and then get back there again to enjoy his suit. Had East covered Q♣ with K♣, declarer could have taken his ace and run the suit without interruption.

It would probably have been better for declarer to play a club to his ace and then a low club and concede a trick to East's king, but it is far from unknown for declarers to have fanciful and over-optimistic ideas and to mis-play a suit. You must ensure that you don't help him.

The third principle then is:

When you can see three touching honour cards, there is no point in covering an honour with your honour since, by doing so, you cannot possibly promote a trick for your side.

Thus there are exceptions to the so-called rule and they are important. Generally, in these situations, you can afford to take your time deciding whether to cover an honour since you will give little away that will be important to the declarer. As you gain experience, you will begin to discern between the times when, by playing low smoothly and appearing disinterested in the trick, you will mislead the declarer, and when you can take your time. For the moment, however, I recommend taking your time whenever you are unsure of which card to play, since you will usually gain more this way. Do not, however, pause when you have only low cards in your hand (even if you are thinking about a signal) since this is against the ethics of the game. To bluff that you have something to think about when you do not is cheating, plain and simple. If that's your bag, take up poker, where you can do that to your heart's content. Incidentally, at bridge, you are permitted to take advantage of your opponents' hesitations, but not your partner's, so do not hesitate for the benefit of your partner, since that too is against the ethics of the game.

Analysing Partner's Lead and Return

Using the lead styles and responses to the lead, as well as the agreements regarding partner's return of the suit led, the defence should be able to formulate the best plan of attack. As always in NTs, the number of tricks available should be counted and checked as the hand progresses. Only when the defence can see that they have sufficient tricks to beat the contract should they cash their winners.

Hand 65   Dealer South

N	E	S	W
–	–	1C	NB
3C	NB	3NT	

```
                    ♠ A7
                    ♥ 632
                    ♦ 963
                    ♣ KQ942
      ♠ 654        ┌─────────┐    ♠ 109832
      ♥ KJ1075     │    N    │    ♥ A4
      ♦ KQ7        │ W     E │    ♦ J10542
      ♣ 103        │    S    │    ♣ 7
                   └─────────┘
                    ♠ KQJ
                    ♥ Q98
                    ♦ A8
                    ♣ AJ865
```

This defence should run simply and smoothly. West leads J♥ – top-of-an-internal-sequence – and East overtakes with his A♥ and returns 4♥. Now, whichever card South plays, West can win, play another top heart and enjoy his two further heart winners. East-West take the first five tricks to beat the contract.

This should look straightforward to you because East is obeying two key principles of defending no-trump contracts. Firstly, he remembers that when partner leads an honour against a NT contract, he should almost always play any honour that he holds immediately and, secondly, East is playing the high card from the shorter holding in the heart suit, to ensure that suit does not block. If he had played small, South would have won and cashed nine more tricks, and East would have been left with the bare A♥.

Hand 66   **Dealer North**

N	E	S	W
NB	NB	1S	NB
2C	NB	3NT	

```
                  ♠ KJ8
                  ♥ K852
                  ♦ 86
                  ♣ Q976
      ♠ 752                      ♠ 643
      ♥ A64          N           ♥ J97
      ♦ KQ1073   W     E         ♦ J92
      ♣ 102          S           ♣ J543
                  ♠ AQ109
                  ♥ Q103
                  ♦ A54
                  ♣ AK8
```

West leads K♦, which must show ♦KQJ or ♦KQ10. East knows that it is the latter and, to show partner that it is safe – and desirable – to continue, East jettisons his J♦. West carries on leading diamonds until A♦ is pushed out, and regains the lead with A♥ to defeat the contract.

When you lead top-of-a-broken-sequence and your partner fails to drop or overtake with an honour card, this marks the unseen honours in the declarer's hand. With this knowledge, you can continue with your suit or switch to another.

Hand 67   Dealer East

N	E	S	W	
–	NB	1C	1H	
1S†	NB	1NT	NB	† *or a Negative Double*
3NT				

```
                      ♠ AQ54
                      ♥ 652
                      ♦ KJ3
                      ♣ J107
      ♠ 973              N              ♠ J1082
      ♥ KQ1094       W     E           ♥ 83
      ♦ 92              S              ♦ A10864
      ♣ A53                            ♣ 92
                      ♠ K6
                      ♥ AJ7
                      ♦ Q75
                      ♣ KQ864
```

When West leads K♥, declarer knows that West's overcall was based on a suit headed by ♥KQ10. To attempt to freeze the suit, declarer will apply the "Bath Coup" (see page 128) which will involve ducking the first trick. This makes it undesirable for West to continue leading hearts since, if he does so, he will provide South with tricks from both his A♥ and J♥.

However, the defence have a counter. East, with no honour card to play, shows his count by playing the higher of his two cards (high card equals an equal number of cards held – see page 99).

West realises that this is two cards (since, if East held four cards, that would leave declarer with only one) and he seeks to find a way to put East on lead to play a heart back to him, through South's ♥AJ holding. Since South has bid clubs and it is almost never right to lead dummy's long suit, West tries a diamond switch, carefully choosing 9♦ to indicate that he has no interest in the suit himself. This hits the jackpot. East wins A♦ and returns 3♥. South only delays the inevitable by playing J♥ and West takes his Q♥. He can now clear the suit with another heart and, when he regains the lead with his A♣, he can cash two further heart tricks to set the contract.

West was indeed lucky to find East with a quick diamond entry but, equally, without the careful card play by both defenders the killing defence would not have been found.

On the next deal, West must remember an adage that is familiar to declarers: retain entries into the hand which contains the long suit you plan to establish. After all, there is little point in establishing winners if you cannot regain the lead in order to enjoy them.

Hand 68   Dealer South

N	E	S	W
–	–	1S	NB
2C	NB	3NT	

West leads 10♦ (top-of-an-internal-sequence); East wins with A♦. East returns the higher of his remaining two cards – 7♦ – and South covers with J♦ or Q♦. With no outside entry, West must duck this trick, retaining his K♦ as his means of access back to his winners – provided East can win a subsequent trick and return the suit to him. When East does regain the lead with A♣, he still has a diamond to lead to West, because West's duck has retained communications between the defenders' hands.

Hand 68   *Dealer South*

```
              ♠ 43
              ♥ K62
              ♦ 64
              ♣ KQJ1084
♠ J652          N          ♠ 1098
♥ J8                       ♥ 109753
♦ K10985    W     E        ♦ A72
♣ 76            S          ♣ A2
              ♠ AKQ7
              ♥ AQ4
              ♦ QJ3
              ♣ 953
```

It is possible that East holds only ♦A7 but, if this is the case, then the declarer started with ♦QJ32 and it would be impossible for East-West to prevail.

Finally, in this group of hands, the defence use their carding understandings to avoid helping the declarer and, in doing so, leave South to fail in a contract which many careless defenders would permit to succeed.

Hand 69   **Dealer South**

N	E	S	W
–	–	1H	NB
1S	NB	1NT	NB
3H†	NB	3NT	

† *forcing, showing 3-card support*

West leads 6♣; East wins A♣ and returns 2♣. This shows that East held only two clubs, so South started with four. South plays 10♣ and West wins with J♣. However, West must not cash his K♣ as this sets up a club trick for South and, anyway, West has no further entry to regain the lead and enjoy his fifth club. As dummy's spades are poor quality and West holds fine intermediates, he switches to 10♠. Now, provided that East holds on to all his hearts (which he should do as South has bid the suit) declarer will find himself a trick short and will, eventually, have to concede defeat.

Hand 69   *Dealer South*

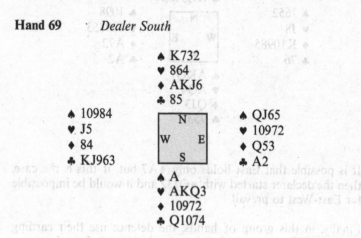

```
                    ♠ K732
                    ♥ 864
                    ♦ AKJ6
                    ♣ 85
   ♠ 10984                        ♠ QJ65
   ♥ J5          N                ♥ 10972
   ♦ 84      W       E            ♦ Q53
   ♣ KJ963        S               ♣ A2
                    ♠ A
                    ♥ AKQ3
                    ♦ 10972
                    ♣ Q1074
```

This hand illustrates two important principles of defence.

Firstly, unless you are certain that by doing so you will establish sufficient tricks to defeat your opponent, you should not cash winners which present the declarer with tricks he could not otherwise make. Here, West's refusal to cash his K♣ prevents South ever from making his Q♣.

Secondly, East must recall the auction in order to confirm that he must protect all four hearts. Each defender has a duty to hang on to cards in suits that are long, either in dummy or in the declarer's hand, to prevent the length of the opponents' suits becoming a trick-making asset. On the hand above, when South shows out of spades on the second round of the suit, East knows that his partner started with four cards headed by ♠109. As a result, East can afford to part with his spades in order to protect his heart holding.

This is a contract that most defenders would allow South to

make. However, by following the basic guidelines and interpreting the messages imparted by the cards played, East-West can prevent South from prevailing. To defeat even a couple of these game contracts each session you play will make a huge difference in your winnings, or your duplicate score.

Using Count to Form your Plan
When you are not involved in trying to win a trick, you should try to show the number of cards you hold in the suit played, by using count signals (see page 99). Your partner can then assess your likely holding and that of the declarer in order to form a picture of the deal and formulate his plan.

Hand 70   Dealer South

N	E	S	W
–	–	1NT	NB
3NT			

♠ Q109
♥ 1094
♦ AK5
♣ KQ74

♠ KJ863   ♠ 742
♥ AQ3   ♥ 872
♦ 108   ♦ QJ76
♣ 832   ♣ 1096

♠ A5
♥ KJ65
♦ 9432
♣ AJ5

West leads 6♠, dummy plays 9♠ and East, unable to contribute positively to the trick, gives count with 2♠ (a low card, showing an odd number). Declarer attacks hearts, leading 10♥ from dummy and letting this run round to West's Q♥. West can count that East is likely to hold three spades and that this leaves South with only one spade left in his hand – the ace. West therefore continues with a low spade and South has to take his ace. To establish the extra tricks he requires, declarer has no choice but to continue attacking hearts and hope desperately that the spades are really 4–4. However, when West takes his A♥, he can cash his three spade winners to defeat the contract.

Notice that without the count signals, West can never work out how many spades South has left and West may decide not risk playing any more spades.

As mentioned earlier, to defeat a no-trump contract, it is usually necessary to continue attacking the suit that has been first led. Here, East could hold a singleton spade and South four cards but, if this is the case, the contract appears unbeatable. For that reason, West should be optimistic that East's 2♠ shows three cards and he defends accordingly.

Perhaps the most vital of all count situations is when there is a long suit in an otherwise entryless dummy. Showing count allows partner to judge when to take his trick.

Hand 71   Dealer South

N	E	S	W	
–	–	2NT†	NB	† 20½ – 22pts
3NT				

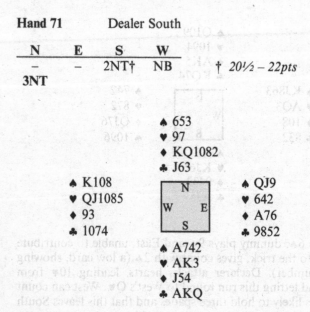

West leads Q♥; East plays 2♥ showing three cards. Declarer wins with K♥ and leads 4♦. West plays 9♦ to show an even number of cards – and it must be two. Now, East must count out the diamond suit. He holds three cards, dummy five and West two cards, so declarer must hold three diamonds. So, East ducks this first trick and again the second time declarer plays diamonds. Now, dummy's diamonds are dead and declarer cannot find his ninth trick. If East takes A♦ earlier, South makes his contract with overtricks.

As well as East confirming his holding in hearts by playing 2♥ at trick one, West's 9♦ count signal proves crucial to the defence, allowing East to judge that he must withhold his A♦ for two rounds, before winning and cutting off declarer from dummy.

There is also one further point here, relevant to the declarer's play. He won the first trick with his K♥ and not A♥. This is the correct play because, if South had held only A♥, he would have held it up (probably in accordance with the Rule of 7 – see page 107). By winning with K♥, he leaves open the possibility that he does not also hold A♥, since it is credible that West led Q♥ from a holding headed by ♥AQJ. By occluding this information, East may not be able to place the remaining cards accurately. Here, however, the meat of the hand was whether East could interpret West's signal in diamonds. He did so, and South failed again.

I'm almost beginning to feel sorry for South in these examples. Each time he ends up in a perfectly reasonable 3NT contract and he gets defeated by East-West. However, I urge you not to feel sorry for your opponents. This is a competitive game and you must remain determined to beat the hell out the opposition at all times – even if you are playing genteel social bridge. And never, ever, fall for opponents' sob stories about how terrible their cards have been. We all have runs of poor cards and we shouldn't expect sympathy then and we shouldn't show any now. Of course, once the game is over, lavish your opponents with praise, tea, cake, alcohol and amateur psychology, but never get suckered into giving them an easy time at the bridge table.

Back to the battle, and it's time to put you in the spotlight again.

See if you can use the clues to fathom out your correct play, as West, on this deal.

Hand 72   Dealer South

N	E	S	W
–	–	1NT	NB
2C†	NB	2D	NB
3NT			† *Stayman*

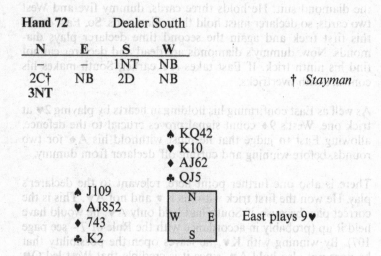

♠ KQ42
♥ K10
♦ AJ62
♣ QJ5

♠ J109
♥ AJ852
♦ 743
♣ K2

East plays 9♥

You decide to lead 5♥. Declarer rises with dummy's K♥ and East plays 9♥. Declarer now leads Q♣, East plays 4♣ and declarer 3♣. You take your K♣ and must now decide what to do.

Take your time to think about the information East has provided, particularly at trick one. Having done that, recall the auction for a dramatic and conclusive clue.

East's 9♥ has indicated an even number of cards held in that suit. It could be two; it could be four. But which? The auction tells you. North used Stayman over South's 1NT opener and South denied holding a 4-card major suit. If East held only two hearts, South would have to hold four himself, and he has announced that he does not. Therefore, East started with four hearts and you should continue by leading A♥. This will fell South's Q♥ and, provided that East continues to play high hearts to avoid a potential blocking of the suit, the rest of the hearts will be yours.

Here is the full deal:

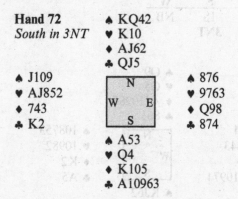

Hand 72
South in 3NT

```
              ♠ KQ42
              ♥ K10
              ♦ AJ62
              ♣ QJ5

♠ J109                        ♠ 876
♥ AJ852          N            ♥ 9763
♦ 743         W     E         ♦ Q98
♣ K2             S            ♣ 874

              ♠ A53
              ♥ Q4
              ♦ K105
              ♣ A10963
```

Again, without the count signal, you would have been guessing what to do. With East's information, you should be able to work out that to play A♥ was correct and then the defence is brutal.

Suit-Preference Signals and Discards
Some players use these signals only against NT contracts but it is easier to apply them against all contracts. Expert players may feel that they give away too much information to the opposition but, for social, club and even congress players, their benefits will outweigh their shortcomings.

SP Signals
Suit-preference signals are used against NT contracts in one key instance: when you are pushing out a stopper from the opponents' hands and you know that your partner will have no cards in that suit to return to you if he gains the lead. In that situation, you want to indicate in which of the other suits your entry lies. In this way, when your partner does gain the lead, he will know how to get you back on lead to cash your winners. Let's see the principle in action.

Hand 73   Dealer South

N	E	S	W
–	–	1S	NB
2D	NB	3NT	

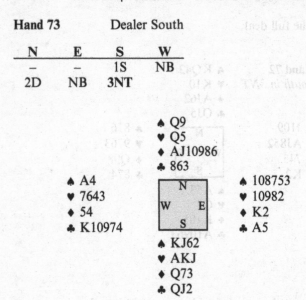

```
                    ♠ Q9
                    ♥ Q5
                    ♦ AJ10986
                    ♣ 863

    ♠ A4                          ♠ 108753
    ♥ 7643            N           ♥ 10982
    ♦ 54          W     E         ♦ K2
    ♣ K10974          S           ♣ A5

                    ♠ KJ62
                    ♥ AKJ
                    ♦ Q73
                    ♣ QJ2
```

West leads 10♣; East wins and returns the suit. West takes his
K♣ and realises that he has only to push out one last stopper
from South. Any club will do, but his choice of card can now
indicate in which suit the re-entry to his hand lies. It is obvious
that diamonds will not be in the picture, since dummy's suit is so
good. He knows, therefore, that East will be wondering whether
West's entry lies in spades or hearts. If West's entry was in hearts
– the lower-ranking suit – he would play his lowest club. As it is,
his entry lies in spades, so he chooses 9♣ – his highest –
indicating the entry in the higher-ranking suit. When East wins
with K♦, despite South having opened 1S, he will use West's
signal to guide him into leading a spade. West wins his A♠ and
cashes his two remaining clubs to set the contract.

Notice that, without the SP Signal, East would almost certainly
have tried leading a heart, since this was an unbid suit. South
would have won, run through his diamond suit and made nine
tricks before West could take his A♠.

SP Discards
Suit-preference discards against NT contracts are used in exactly the same way as against suit contracts: the first time that a defender cannot follow suit, he throws away a card in the suit he is least interested in his partner leading. If he wants the higher ranking of the remaining two suits (that is to say, not the suit of which he has run out, nor the suit he has discarded) he plays a high card in the suit he does not want. If he wants the lower-ranking of the remaining suits, he plays the lowest card in the suit he does not want. Let's see it in action.

Hand 74   Dealer North

N	E	S	W
1C	NB	1D	NB
1H	NB	**3NT**	

                ♠ 94
                ♥ AK94
                ♦ 10
                ♣ AQ9762

♠ Q10862   ♠ J75
♥ 865   N   ♥ 1073
♦ AK98   W   E   ♦ J54
♣ 3   S   ♣ K854

                ♠ AK3
                ♥ QJ2
                ♦ Q7632
                ♣ J10

West leads 6♠ to East's J♠ and South's K♠. Declarer leads J♣ and, when West follows small, East ducks. The reason for that duck will be explained shortly. South leads 10♣ and West can now discard. He knows that South still holds A♠ – since East would have played it at trick one if he had held it – and he can see ♥AK in dummy. There also appear to be five club tricks available for declarer. To defeat the contract, then, East-West must take four more tricks immediately, once East wins his K♣.

Only diamonds offer this prospect. To indicate to East that he wants a diamond led, West discards 2♠, confirming that he does not want a spade returned and indicating that he wants the lower-ranking remaining suit. East takes his K♣ and, instead of returning his partner's suit as he would usually, he takes note of West's 2♠ discard and decides to lead a diamond. Since he can see the singleton 10♦ in dummy, East decides to lead his J♦ to pin dummy's ten beneath it. Now, South is in big trouble. If he covers East's J♦ with his queen, West wins and cashes three more diamond tricks; if declarer ducks, East is still on lead and can pump another diamond through South's hand. If South plays low again, West wins with 9♦ and cashes his ♦AK; if instead South plays Q♦ this time, again West can win and enjoy two more diamond winners.

To defeat this contract, West had to dissuade East from returning the suit he led originally. He did this by choosing to discard a spade – the suit he least wants East to lead – straight away. The fact that it was a low spade indicated an interest in the lower-ranking suit out of diamonds and hearts. Despite the fact that South had bid diamonds, East obeyed, noted dummy's singleton 10♦ and played the only card that could defeat the contract.

Let's return to East's refusal to win the first club trick when South led his J♣. Why would he do that?

> *Defending NT contracts, it is generally right not to win at your first opportunity if the declarer is attacking a long suit and you know that he will finesse again.*

Here, the result of ducking the first club trick proved crucial. South repeated the play by leading 10♣ and, this time, West had run out of the suit and could make a SP discard. This discard led to the killing switch from East which he would almost certainly not have found if West had not had the chance to signal. So, one reason not to win the trick immediately when declarer is finessing in his long suit is to get information from your partner, should he be able to signal on a later round.

Another reason might be in an attempt to exhaust either declarer or dummy of his supply of the suit in order to cut communications between your opponents' two hands.

A final benefit is that, by not winning the first time the declarer finesses, your opponent may place your partner with the missing honour rather than you. If he bases his plan on the fact that the finesse is working, he may reject another line of play which would have been more successful. To put it more simply: by not revealing where the missing honour lies, you keep declarer guessing.

It is important that you play low smoothly because, if you hesitate, you will reveal the position and most of the benefits of refusing the trick will be lost. This is something that you should think about when dummy first appears and the declarer is making his plan. If declarer is one of those impudent, rash types who starts playing without even considering his predicament, don't be hurried into playing. Just put your cards face down on the table, smile sweetly and declare, "You're too fast for me", and consider the likely course of the hand. You are fully entitled to take your time and no amount of tut-tutting or finger-tapping should put you off. When you are ready, pick up your hand again and continue to play.

Incidentally, I have met only two players in my life who could start playing – and play perfectly – without seeming to think. One is no longer in this world; the other you may conceivably encounter amongst the highest echelons of the game. No one else is nearly clever enough so, if your friends play without thought, they are just that: thoughtless. You will get the better of them for sure, sooner or later.

The exception to the guideline about not winning at the first opportunity when declarer is finessing in his long suit would be when, by taking the trick, you defeat the contract, or when you know that by winning it, you or your partner can definitely cash the setting trick.

Lead-Directing Doubles
Although, clearly, this is a bidding matter, it is worth noting these agreements concerning lead-directing doubles against no-trump contracts. There are two situations and, because it is

so frustrating for your partner when you do not recognize them, they are worth learning.

Hand 75   Dealer South

N	E	S	W
–	–	1D	NB
1H	NB	1NT	NB
3NT	Dbl		

North-South reach 3NT on a standard auction and, suddenly, East doubles. This asks for a heart lead.

> *When partner doubles a NT contract after suits have been bid, it asks you to lead dummy's first bid suit.*

The hand might look like this:

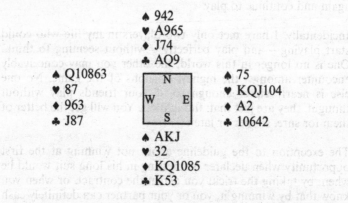

Without East's double, West would probably lead 6♠. Declarer would win with J♠, push out East's A♦ and claim eleven tricks. However, when East doubles, asking West to lead dummy's bid suit, the defence goes rather differently. After a lead-directing double, it is nearly always correct to lead the highest card in the suit you have been asked to lead. So, West leads 8♥ and East will continue to play hearts until declarer parts with dummy's ace. When South tackles diamonds, East will take his ace immediately and cash his remaining heart winners. The defence will make four heart tricks and A♦ and defeat the contract.

The second situation is rare, but crops up from time to time. When this hand first occurred, West did not know the meaning of his partner's double and spent many angst-ridden minutes trying to decide what to lead. After much deep thought, he led the wrong suit and his opponents got a great result.

Hand 76   Dealer South

N	E	S	W	
–	–	1NT†	NB	† Strong NT, 15–18pts
3NT	Dbl			

```
                    ♠ K96
                    ♥ 843
                    ♦ A6
                    ♣ K6432
      ♠ J10742                    ♠ 83
      ♥ 7              N          ♥ AKQJ5
      ♦ J8          W   E        ♦ 97542
      ♣ J10975         S          ♣ 8
                    ♠ AQ5
                    ♥ 10962
                    ♦ KQ103
                    ♣ AQ
```

West can work out that his partner holds approximately 10–12 points but no one should ever double a freely bid 3NT contract simply because they hold points, since this would give away their position and enhance the declarer's chance of success. So, this double must again be lead-directing. Unfortunately, when this hand was first played, West did not know for which suit the double was asking and so led what he hoped would be a safe J♣. Unfortunately, declarer then wrapped up the next ten tricks to record a doubled overtrick.

When partner doubles a NT contract in which no suits have been bid during the auction, it asks you to lead your shorter major suit.

This is because, since your opponents have not invoked Stayman, it is unlikely that they have a major suit fit and it is possible that your partner has a solid source of tricks in one major suit. If partner's points are concentrated in just one suit, the declarer is likely to make sufficient tricks quickly in the other three suits. This is why it is so important to attract the correct lead from partner.

On the hand above, West should lead 7♥ and his partner will take the first five tricks to defeat the contract.

Incidentally, making lead-directing doubles is all very well but, when your partner fails to lead your suit, reserve your criticism until you are aware of the full deal. Years ago, I failed to lead my partner's requested suit during a hard-fought inter-club match and the noises emanating from across the table sounded like the beginnings of a volcanic eruption. Only once declarer had claimed his contract and revealed his hand did it dawn on my partner that I was, in fact, void in the suit he was so desperate for me to lead!

7

FINAL WORDS

As you introduce new elements into your bridge game, it is inevitable that you will make mistakes and make yourself and your partnership look foolish. Be sure you are playing with an understanding, mature, partner who can take the mild embarrassment of looking a bit silly from time to time and take the longer view that it is all in the spirit of trying to improve. I can't tell you how many stupid mistakes I've made over the years and, I have to say, those are the moments from which you learn the most. However, once you see the points you are studying pay dividends – and you will – you will never forget them. Slowly but surely, your results will begin to improve and the respect your opponents show you will increase. That is the time when your confidence will begin to grow and it is a great feeling.

I do think that to play even social bridge well you have to put in some reading and plenty of good quality practice. By that I mean that you should stick to one bidding system and one or two authors on play and disregard those authors who claim that they will make you experts if you glance at their texts. Keep trying to picture all four hands at the table, however difficult that may, at first, seem. It is the key to transforming your game and, once you master it, it is a skill that will never leave you. When practising try to play either with players better than you who do not mind quietly advising you when you go wrong, or with a regular group of friends with whom you can discuss hands after they have been played. Keeping the cards in front of you, duplicate style, is a great way to play because, whenever declarer or defence feel that they might have done better, the hand can be re-created so that individuals can check on themselves. Note: on themselves, not on their partners! If you play with people who tell you that this would spoil their game, I'd cut down how often you play with them. Clearly they don't want to improve and they don't want you to either. Perhaps they rather enjoy telling you what you should have done once all the cards have disappeared into an anonymous pile in the middle of the table and you can't check their analysis. Keeping the cards will cut down on gratuitous comment from others at the table and, by threatening to reveal the evidence, will ensure that everyone concentrates a bit harder on the game.

And that's the crux of it all: concentration. If you play bridge with friends for fun, that's fine. I'm not one for idle gossip, catching up on soap-opera plots or speculating on the love-life of the local bridge club captain (though I am not adverse to putting the world to rights) but, if that's your bag, do it between bridge hands. Even if you only play four deals in an afternoon or evening (or morning), at least concentrate while you play them, otherwise you might as well be playing Old Maid.

I firmly believe that you enjoy bridge more as you improve. Since none of us will be anywhere near perfect, it is a wonderful challenge, and a brilliant antidote to the pitiful offerings of a mind-numbing, sensationalist media. Above all, have fun while you play because, no matter how ambitious I may be for all my readers, it is still just a game.

GLOSSARY

This section includes definitions for some terms which appear in this book with which you may not be familiar. If you feel uncertain about further terms, you should find them defined within the section in which they appear. Failing that, you may wish to consult my *Bridge for Complete Beginners* which defines all the basic bridge terms.

block; blocking; blockage
To leave yourself with winning cards in one of your partnership's hands with no means of gaining access to that hand, either in the suit being played or in other suits.

cash, cashing
To take winning tricks.

Chicago
A style of playing and scoring bridge, where you play a set of four hands, with differing pre-set vulnerabilities. At the end of the four hands, it is traditional to swap partners. Chicago is often played when there are five or six players as it allows four hands to be played, the scores noted, and extra players to enter the game.

draw trumps/play out trumps
To draw trumps is to pull the trumps from the opponents' hands until they hold no more. To play out the trump suit might involve continuing to lead the trump suit even once the opponents have none left, with the intention of pressurizing the opponents into discarding a card helpful to the declarer.

duck, ducking
To refuse to win a trick when you have the option of doing so.

Duplicate (sometimes known as Duplicate bridge, or Pairs)
The competitive form of the game where the same hands travel around multiple tables and the results are calculated on how well you fare on each deal compared to the other players at other tables.

endplay
An advanced manoeuvre that usually occurs towards the end of the play, in which you allow an opponent to gain the lead so that what he leads is to your benefit and increases your chances of making extra tricks. There are several variations.

entry, entries
Card or cards which provide a means of access into your own hand or into your partner's hand.

"I didn't have an entry" would mean that you had no high card which provided you with a chance to gain or re-gain the lead.

exit, exiting
To lose the lead deliberately, often into one chosen opponent's hand, with the intention of endplaying them. (See Endplay, above.)

finesse and 2-way finesse
To attempt to win a trick with a card lower than one held by your opponent. For example if, between the declarer's hand and dummy, these were the holdings:

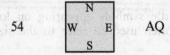

54   AQ

The correct play for declarer would be to lead a low card from West and, when North follows with a small card, to play the queen from the East hand. If North holds the king, your queen will win the trick. If South holds the king, your queen will lose. This represents a 50% chance of making a cheap trick.

A 2-way finesse is one which can be taken through either opponent. For example:

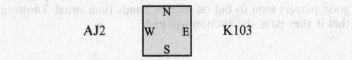

AJ2   K103

If you thought (perhaps from the auction or from the early play of the cards) that North held the queen, you could lead low from West and, when North played low, you could win the trick by playing the ten from East. If North did hold the queen, your ten would win the trick cheaply. If, on the other hand, you thought that South held the queen, you could lead 3 from the East hand and, when South played low, you could win cheaply by playing the jack from the West hand.

loser
A card which, on correct defence from the opposition, and without the influence of trumps, would lose to a higher card during the play of the hand.

master/top trump
The highest trump outstanding.

peter
The play of two cards by a player on successive tricks, which imparts a message about his hand.

pips
The number of little symbols appearing on low cards (two through to ten), often used to refer to the size of the low cards.

pitch
To throw away, discard

protective position
During the auction, this refers to a player whose left hand opponent has made a bid, followed by two passes (from his partner and from his right hand opponent). In this position, good players tend to bid on weaker hands than usual, knowing that if they pass, the auction will end.

pull
As in "to pull trumps" – to draw out.

relay bid
A meaningless bid one partner uses simply to ensure that the auction continues and his partner gets a further chance to bid. Often used after a 2C or very strong opening bid to ensure that the opener can describe his hand further.

Roman Key-Card Blackwood
This is a variation on the traditional 4NT Blackwood, ace-asking convention. In RKCB, both the king and queen of trumps can be included in the inquiry and kings can be cue-bid on the way to a grand slam. RKCB is also known as "Key Card Blackwood" or "Five Ace Blackwood".

ruff/trump
To ruff and to trump are interchangeable terms. Ruff was the original old-fashioned term, still widely in use today.

set, setting trick
To set the contract is to defeat it; the setting trick is the trick which defeats the contract.

squeeze (pseudo-squeeze)
You are squeezed when you have two good elements in your hand but, because you are being forced to discard, you must eventually unguard one of these features. Set up correctly by an expert opponent, a squeeze should ensure that whatever you decide to throw away will prove disastrous for you.

A pseudo-squeeze is where you feel that you are squeezed but, had you had detailed knowledge of the other hands, you would have been able to find a safe discard in one of your suits.

Claiming that "I was squeezed" is a favourite excuse for poor players who have not been following the play and do not know which cards to hang onto and which to throw away. A squeeze (or pseudo-squeeze) is a rare occurrence, most unlikely to make an appearance in any but the most advanced games.

Teams of Four
A competitive form of the game, based on Duplicate bridge, where you play as part of a four-man team. One partnership sits North-South at one table, the other East-West at the other table. Your opponents do likewise. The same hands are played at both tables and the scores are compared to find the winners.

touching cards
Cards in sequence, for example 987.

underlead
"Never underlead an ace against a suit contract" means never to lead away from a suit headed by an ace. For example: A753 – to lead any low card from this suit would be to underlead the ace.

By the same author

BRIDGE FOR COMPLETE BEGINNERS

Paul Mendelson assumes that you start with no knowledge of the game at all. He takes you through the key basic principles so that you learn about the Acol system of bidding and how to play a hand, both as declarer and in defence. Once you have mastered the book, you should have reached the standard of a good 'social' player.

THE RIGHT WAY TO PLAY BRIDGE

With Paul Mendelson's help you can improve your game at a social, or competitive, level. You will learn to plan and reassess your campaign step-by-step and calculate with precision who holds which cards. You will also discover when to obstruct with bluff and bombast, how to pinpoint best leads and steal the best contracts, and ways to think strategically under pressure.

In the same series

THE NEW MAHJONG

The game of mahjong (sparrow), also known as the game of Four Winds, is derived from traditional Chinese card games. Lacking any international authority, it has up to the present been played in scores of different ways throughout the world.

In 1998 the Chinese government declared mahjong to be an official sport and published a unique set of rules, defining 81 scoring hands and designed to standardize the game throughout the country. In 2002 these rules were adopted in the first World Championship, held in Tokyo, which attracted players from many countries and they were formally declared to be the official rules for all future international events.

Previous forms of the game will in time inevitably be replaced by the new mahjong. In this book, D B Pritchard explains the 81 scoring hands and the rules governing them. It is, therefore, as well as being ideal for beginners, essential reading for mahjong players everywhere.